THE ART OF WRITING DRAMA

Michelene Wandor

Methuen Drama

Published by Methuen Drama

1 3 5 7 9 10 8 6 4 2

First published 2008
Methuen Drama
A & C Black Publishers Limited
38 Soho Square
London W1D 3HB
www.acblack.com

A CIP catalogue record for this book is available from the British Library

ISBN 978 0 413 77586 3

Typeset in 10pt Janson Text by SX Composing DTP, Rayleigh, Essex
Printed and bound in Great Britain by CPI Cox & Wyman, Reading, RG1 8EX

The Art of Writing Drama

Michelene Wandor is a playwright, poet, fiction writer and musician. Her dramatisation of *The Wandering Jew* was produced at the National Theatre in 1987, the same year her adaptation of *The Belle of Amherst* won an International Emmy for Thames TV. Her prolific radio work includes original plays and dramatisations (novels by Dostoyevsky, Jane Austen, George Eliot, Kipling, Sara Paretsky, Margaret Drabble and D. H. Lawrence), many nominated for Sony and Prix Italia Awards. Her books on contemporary theatre include *Carry On, Understudies* and *Post-War British Drama: Looking Back in Gender*. She has published a number of short-story collections. *Musica Transalpina* was a Poetry Book Society Recommendation for 2006 and her dramatic poem, *The Music of the Prophets* (both Arc Publications), was supported by a grant from the European Association for Jewish Culture. Since 2004 she has held a Royal Literary Fund Fellowship. Her history of creative writing in the UK, *The Author is not Dead, Merely Somewhere Else: Creative Writing Reconceived*, was published in 2008. Her new play, *Tulips in Winter*, about Spinoza, will be broadcast on Radio 3 in 2008.

Contents

Author; the Death of the Author and the fourth wall;
audience as active; conclusions

The director; the performer, acting and the text; the
fourth wall; after Stanislavsky – new objectivism;
conclusions: performance and immediacy

Size matters; narrative voice, point of view, character and
subjectivity; poly-vocality and the dialogic; narrative,
structure and causality

Early workshop history; the tutorial precedent; workshop
pedagogy; authority; workshop practice and power-
relations; criticism and value judgement; training
professional writers versus self-expression; the workshop as
a House of Correction; the workshop as therapy group;
theatre workshops; conclusions

Action or character?; action, conflict and crisis (actions
speak louder than words); character; premise, idea, vision,
theme; scenario; dialogue; narrative and causality; drama
and creative writing; conclusions – dialogue – the absent
centre

Main or subsidiary; from directions to performance; extra-
dialogic stage directions; extra- and intra-dialogic stage
directions; conclusions

Introduction

This book is about the art of writing drama. The statement sounds more straightforward than it actually is. The 'art' refers to the position of drama as one of the performance arts. 'Writing' refers to a skill and understanding of conventions which are distinctive to the dramatist, and which have symbiotic links with other imaginative literature – poetry and prose fiction, all covered by the now widely used phrase 'creative writing'. The overarching term 'drama' is Janus-like: looking in two directions at once. It gestures towards the written and/or published text on the one hand, and to the complexity of performance and applied technical approaches to production on the other. These two interdependent artistic practices result in a combined product (the performance/artefact, live or recorded) and the discrete written product in the text on the page (sometimes, but not always, published in book form). The two are generally distinguished by the terms 'dramatic text' and 'performance text'.

Learning to write drama

Drama comes to us via a number of technologically distinctive media: theatre, radio, television and film. It is read, seen, enjoyed and studied in many different contexts. Drama schools train performers, technical staff and, more recently, have provided opportunities for students interested in becoming directors. Set and costume design can be studied at art schools, and film schools provide training courses for the technologically intensive forms of recorded drama. However, all these have addressed the skills of writing drama to a much more limited extent.

In universities, Theatre Studies were invigorated in the last part of the twentieth century by the development of Performance Studies. Influenced by anthropology, cultural theory and semiology, this new subject illuminated the complex, intertwined ways in which meanings are created in performance. Performance Studies exist alongside, or have been incorporated into, more traditional university drama degrees, which study the histories of theatre and published plays. However, here too, the actual writing of drama has rarely been included as a distinct practice, with its own history and theory.

This is not to say that writing drama is unpopular: quite the opposite. Theatres, radio, television and film companies are inundated with scripts from aspiring writers. The vast majority of these – an estimated 95 per cent – are rejected, but enthusiasm persists. The thriving amateur theatre movement in the UK not only devotes itself to staging productions of established plays, but also has a large appetite for drama specially written for amateur production. In adult education and community-based writing courses across the country, writing drama is a strong presence.

Since the late 1960s there has been much more stress on the development of new writing, in particular for theatre. Occasional residencies for playwrights enable developing writers to work in theatres, and for dramaturgs/directors to support, and often produce, their writing. Some theatres run 'workshops' for new drama and organise staged readings for new work. Many theatres have educational outreach activities, including Theatre-in-Education, where there are opportunities for 'devising' new drama, with input from local communities, teachers and the company, to select subject matter and be more closely involved with the writing process. In recent years BBC radio, the largest drama-commissioning organisation in the world (some 1,000 dramas each year), has also set up new writers' initiatives. Film schools include writing specifically for film as one of the skills students can acquire.

There is thus some opportunity for those who want to write drama to learn within the industry, as it were. Of course, this can be very rewarding. Producers, directors and artistic directors may be sensitive readers and genuinely interested in developing 'talent', but inevitably the extent to which this can be done is relatively limited. Theatres and production companies are primarily there to *produce* work which will enable their survival, economic and artistic, even if publicly subsidised. Education is not their primary purpose. Most directors are not *writers*, and their expertise lies in the way they read and respond to already written drama. This responsiveness to text is vital; in a context where work is devised with companies, any would-be writer is bound to learn a great deal about what other theatre workers bring to their work. However, writing is a distinctive skill in its own right. Industrial apprenticeship of this kind can be helpful, and should continue. However, it is now timely to extend the way in which writing drama is thought about, understood and practised.

This book is positioned in relation to all the various ways in which the art of writing drama may be developed and learned. It is not, in any way, a replacement for those who may devise work with companies or directors to develop their writing in relation to the practicalities and imperatives of theatre production and performance. This book augments those hands-on processes, by enabling students and writers to stand back from the immediate practical pressures, to become aware of the place of drama in the performance and literary worlds, and to think about what is involved in their own developing practice of writing drama. It is written out of the experience and thinking of a dramatist, and from a passionate conviction that writing drama is a writerly skill in its own right – its relationship to performance-in-production is what gives it a different complexion from writing for publication as poetry and prose fiction are. In particular, this book has been spurred by the establishment of a new area of study in higher education – creative writing.

Creative writing and drama

The rapidly expanding field of creative writing (CW) degrees has, in principle, provided a context within which dramatic writing could be fully addressed in higher education. However, at both under- and postgraduate level, prose fiction and poetry dominate. Drama, where it is present at all, is most often taught in the form of screen- or the rather more ambiguously titled 'script-writing' courses. The fact that the first MA in Playwriting in this country was set up in 1989 at the University of Birmingham contrasts with the first MA in Creative Writing (in the novel), set up in 1970 at the University of East Anglia. This captures the time and culture lag in addressing the art of writing drama in formal higher education.

In recent years the advent of creative writing in universities, at both under- and postgraduate levels, has generated a considerable number of 'how-to' books, which aim to provide practical advice on different kinds of imaginative writing. These are not, strictly speaking, written as classroom textbooks. Most of them are addressed to individuals, to the self-help writing market, as it were. In keeping with the relatively minor place of drama in creative writing, there have been fewer books on writing drama.

This book is part of that new development, but it sets out to do something rather different, provocatively complementary to what is already available. The new contexts for studying dramatic writing as a practice provide opportunities to explore the insights of performance theory, cultural and language studies, and to discuss how they might contribute to a new approach to dramatic pedagogy. At the same time the practical imperatives of production and performance remain acutely relevant to approaches to teaching the art of writing drama in higher education. This makes the idea of teaching dramatic writing separate from performance conditions (i.e., away from access to theatres and other forms of production) complicated in ways which are different from the conditions which apply to teaching poetry and prose fiction. However, I would argue that it is possible to do so. I will also argue that the conventions of the academic 'workshop', in which creative writing is predominantly taught, are unsatisfactory and need to be reconceived.

In other words the book offers a framework for the practice of writing drama, by historicising, theorising and critiquing its pedagogical context and procedures, and then by proposing alternative methodologies. I have set out to explore and deconstruct some commonly held assumptions which underlie most of the current approaches to writing drama, and which, as I shall argue, impede a real understanding of the dramatist's working process *as writer*, and therefore affect pedagogic approaches to teaching dramatic writing. Based on a combination of this analysis and my own teaching experience over nearly three decades, I suggest some alternative approaches and methods.

Backgrounds

I first taught a playwriting course in the early 1980s, at the Guildhall School of Music and Drama in London. I was already a professional writer, earning my living from plays, poetry and journalism. I began writing for the theatre in the early 1970s, expanding into short stories, radio drama and some television by the end of the decade. My first plays were produced in the early 1970s in the fringe theatre, which burgeoned after official censorship was abolished in 1968. I also worked as poetry editor and theatre reviewer on the (then) new *Time Out* magazine.

I have always written in all three core fictional genres – drama, poetry and prose fiction. I have also always reviewed all three genres and written non-fiction studies of contemporary theatre. My passion for writing drama was matched in the 1970s by my sense of urgency about the importance of documenting this new writing. As a woman dramatist I was, along with other women working in the theatre, concerned about the relatively small number of women in executive and artistic positions, particularly as writers. This will be discussed further in chapter 14. Things may have improved a little on the gender-balance front, but only a little. We are still a long way from parity between male and female playwrights.

The 'political' or 'alternative' socialist, art school derived, gay and feminist theatres of the 1970s put onstage new content, new experiences, new ideas, from all sides challenging twentieth-century performance traditions. It was exciting and controversial in its writing, performance, venues and audiences. It continued a tradition of radicalism already there in the theatre of the 1950s, with the work of (among many others) Joan Littlewood, at the Theatre Royal in London's Stratford East. Commercial theatres benefited too, not only in transferring successful productions, but in adopting some of the innovations in fluid, non-naturalistic staging. Some writers and performers who began in fringe theatre later developed careers in radio, TV and film. The new venues and audiences enabled great variety and vitality in new writing.[1]

---

[1] *Disrupting the Spectacle* by Peter Ansorge (Pitman, 1975); *The Arts Britain Ignores* by Naseem Khan (Arts Council of Great Britain, 1976); *Dreams and Deconstructions* edited by Sandy Craig (Amber Lane Press, 1980); *Stages in the Revolution* by Catherine Itzin (Eyre Methuen, 1980); *Understudies: theatre and sexual politics* by Michelene Wandor (Methuen, 1981), expanded and revised as *Carry on, Understudies* (Routledge, 1986); *Look Back in Gender: sexuality and the family in post-war British Drama* by Michelene Wandor (Methuen, 1987), revised and expanded as *Post-War British Drama: Looking Back in Gender* (Routledge, 2001).

After censorship

After the repeal of official theatre censorship in Britain in 1968, plays no longer had to be submitted to the Lord Chamberlain for approval, before they could be rehearsed and staged. Even after a script had been approved, representatives from the Lord Chamberlain's office might well visit the theatre incognito, to make sure no untoward *ad libs* or other changes had crept into the production. Theatre censorship has had a long history. Performance, as a particular kind of group activity, gives theatre a high-profile public presence, rather different from the relatively individuated worlds of book reading.

Until the late 1960s, therefore, there were strict controls applied to representations of royalty onstage, important historical figures, explicit references to sexuality, nudity, potentially blasphemous content and the censorship of 'bad' language. These strictures could be bypassed if theatres were set up as clubs, with membership, and it was in these circumstances that much radical work was staged while censorship was still in force.[2]

It is extraordinary (and salutary) to realise that writing for the theatre has only had the same freedoms accorded to the novel and poetry for about half a century. The post-censorship theatrical landscape not only helped transform who wrote and performed what, where it was performed and to whom, but tacitly now made it possible to teach dramatic writing with more flexible expectations of what a play should or could be.

During the 1970s a whole range of new dramatic phenomena came into being: writing, venues, studio spaces, styles of performance, touring companies who performed plays in community halls, in schools, pubs, basements – anywhere with a space and an audience. Called 'fringe', 'alternative', 'underground', 'political', it was closely influenced by, and linked with, the cultural and political

[2] See 'The Royal Smut-Hound' by Kenneth Tynan, in *Post-War British Drama: Looking Back in Gender*, pp. 98–111.

movements of the time: socialism, feminism, the gay movement, avant-garde artistic experiments in poetry, performance art and theatre, often incorporating moves to democratise theatre-making and theatre-going. The performance-art wing of this movement focused on work which privileged a theatrical *mis-en-scène* in which improvisation and physical theatre put the written text, or verbal language itself, into the background.

Paradoxically, the 1970s and 1980s were decades in which a tension, sometimes creative, sometimes not, affected opportunities for, and attitudes to, writing drama. On the one hand post-censorship theatre provided new opportunities. Politics and art, the changing demography of the UK, all introduced new voices, new imaginative worlds to the theatre, TV and film. At the same time sections of the political theatre movement privileged democratised working practices, challenging what was seen as the traditional, putatively tyrannical, authority of the individual dramatist and director.

Cinema theory (in particular the development of *auteur* theory), as well as Performance Studies, focused on the 'visual' media of film and TV, as well as on stage performance, analysing the way meanings were created and conveyed through non-verbal means. Somewhere within all these the dramatist was being moved around, re-placed or replaced, displaced, challenged and sometimes just dismissed.

Positioning dramatic writing

Writing drama is suspended between the ideological frameworks which conceptualise the writer and writing, and the needs, skills and aptitudes which belong to those who realise their work in performance. Institutionally, it is sometimes encouraged by dramaturgs attached to theatres specialising in new writing; it is sometimes taught as part of creative writing courses; it is often a popular element in adult education. The actual teaching is not necessarily linked to the practicalities and skills of production. The art of writing drama raises some very distinctive pedagogical questions about the relationship between the dramatic text and the performance text.

The relationship between writing and reviewing drama works differently, by comparison with the novel and poetry. While it is common for novelists and poets to review each others' books and write critical studies, in drama matters are not so straightforward. A playwright reviewing productions is assessing the work of other applied skills, as well as those of fellow playwrights. Drama critics rarely venture into the world of writing and greasepaint – and so, expert and knowledgeable as they aim to be in responding to what goes on onstage or on the screen, they rarely have any working experience or involvement on the other side of the footlights. In his still provocative book *The Empty Space* (first published in 1968), director Peter Brook pointed out that some of the most vibrant playwrights of that decade – John Arden, John Osborne, Arnold Wesker – had been performers and directors before they became writers. A wide range of drama-related experiences can be a great advantage for a dramatist.

This is not to say, of course, that everyone who writes drama must also be a fully-fledged professional in another part of the process. Nor, it should be stressed, does it mean that a consummate performer, director or designer, however subtly aware of the nuances of text and staging, can automatically write drama – well or at all. Like all other applied skills, writing is its own skill. It takes time to learn and develop.

However, there is no doubt that anyone studying the art and practice of writing drama – for whatever medium – should, over time, acquire an understanding and practical experience of the nature of rehearsal, preparation for performance and the potentials of appropriate technologies. Even though a dramatist may never perform or direct, the demands and imperatives of these skills need to be internalised in a way which enhances and stimulates the imagination in relation to the conventions of the dramatic form. Like all other CW students, those who study the practical art of writing drama need an acquired understanding of the written conventions available to them. This should ideally involve the study of written texts, history and theory, as well as the development of a variety of analytical responses to performance – all these feed back into the imagination to enable the dramatist to know more sharply and clearly what it is to write multi-voiced texts, which have an extra dimension in performance. The novelist or poet can be involved in publication, in terms of cover design, and/or the layout on the page, but that is, generally, as far as it goes. 'Publication' for the dramatist means not only the appearance of the text in printed form, but the third dimension of public distribution through performance, in the presence of live audiences.

From imagination to page and stage

This makes the pedagogy of writing drama (teaching and learning) particularly complex, since classroom-based writing is inevitably divorced from the technologies of stage, TV, radio and film. However, this very partiality can have a great advantage, highlighting one of the most important arguments of this book. I maintain that in order to apply drama-writing skills to *any* of the performance media, students must acquire understanding and experience in two discrete and related processes. First, writing drama must be approached as a literary, practice-based form – from imagination to page. Second, students need to acquire direct experience of the nature of performance in space and time, in relation to their own writing – from page to stage. The combination of these two, gradually, cumulatively, enables students to begin to understand and put into practice what is involved in the journey from imagination to page to stage. It entails a training in understanding what happens in their own imaginations, as well as an understanding of the range of dramatic conventions available to them, and the potentialities of performance.

In this context the drama-writing classroom can be transformed. To borrow from Peter Brook, I can take any empty classroom and make it into a stage. Moving between writing and performance in the classroom provides an opportunity to re-create many of the conditions of performance without the pressures. Alongside the writing process, students can begin to gain a sense of what happens when the words come off the page and into the air. In the classroom drama is voiced, embodied, performed, seen and heard, then returned to the page, where it moves back into the imagination and the whole process starts again. The writing moves in time and space in genre-specific ways, only available in a pedagogic experience, in a group, in the immediacy of the classroom, where the imperatives of time and space establish their distinctive relationship to the writing on the page.

Writing drama per se – the complete text

This book argues that a course in drama writing per se provides a foundation from which students can go on and apply their writing specifically to the stage, film/TV/radio drama-making processes. It posits writing drama as a text-centred process, while also taking fully into account other contingent and necessary processes. The ephemeral and infinitely analysable immediacy of live performance in the 'present' moment of the classroom can interrogate the interface between writing, production and reception, and, with enough time, can investigate ways in which each dramatic medium can have an impact on the imagination, as well as on the writing. A course in 'writing drama' *as such* is, therefore, a foundation course in the most important sense: without a secure foundation, all the tips, exercises and writing to formula risk being symptomatic rather than fundamental to the pedagogic process. Going back to basic principles and stating the very obvious, the dramatist writes. That is all the dramatist does. That is everything the dramatist does. He/she does nothing else. Teaching dramatic writing cannot be done from the point of view or perspective of performance or production, and cannot adequately be taught, I would argue, by directors, however invaluable their own particular responses to text may be.

The Death of the Author and the birth of the dramatist

The argument that writing drama is a skill in its own right and not secondary to, or subsumed within, performance, resonates against what has become one of the most powerful conceits of our cultural time. In 1967 French theorist, Roland Barthes, pronounced the Death of the Author.[3] The tension between the actual responsibility of the dramatist, the practicalities of performance, the notion of the death of the author along with the insights of semiology into the meaning-creating processes of drama must all be addressed for anyone interested in the art of writing drama. The conceit of the 'death of the author' fits neatly into the foregrounding of Performance Studies and the insistence of the drama industries that writing is only one of a number of elements in the process of production. Barthes's theory (along with his other writings) has remained an implicit and explicit rubric, which still hovers behind much contemporary critical analysis and this is at odds with the newly stressed focus on authorship, which emerges from Creative Writing courses. Steering a path through all this, what follows presents a newly radicalised argument for the discrete nature of writing drama as an individual authorial practice (intertextuality and social context notwithstanding).

[3] 'The Death of the Author' by Roland Barthes, in *Image, Music, Text* (Fontana Press, 1977).

Drama – the 'complete' text

This leads to something all professional dramatists know. In the vast majority of cases, even where there is discussion with the director, some rewriting during rehearsal processes, the writer of drama for any medium fundamentally completes her/his work before the work of other people (i.e., the production process) has begun; conceptually, formally, imaginatively and on the page. An entire working process, which might take years, has been completed before the written text exists and those who work on its production come into contact with it. The generally inadequate understanding of this derives from a number of factors and conditions, all of which will be discussed in due course in this book. Even in devised drama, where one person is in charge of the writing, there is still crucial conceptual and imaginative work which is 'authored', to a lesser or greater extent, by the individual concerned.

Imaginative writing, in all genres, is a specific mode of thought. Thinking and imagining are invisible individuated processes, although they derive from, depend on and feed back into historically and socially constructed and shared conventions. Through the deployment of these, words are written and organised, subject to an understanding of the conventions of the chosen form. In relation to writing drama these conventions involve a relationship with staging/production, but these are separate (and separated in practice) parts of the process. Even where drama is co-devised and/or co-written, the moments where writing is done still engage with the individual realisation (in the mind and on the page) of a cultural convention.

The dramatist's active and ultimately executive relationship and responsibility remain towards the written text. This will be discussed in relation to concepts of authorship and copyright. It will also take into account aspects of performance theory and the division of labour in the industrial process of producing drama. It is a complicated argument, but without a degree of clarity the work of the dramatist (and thus the pedagogic process) remains hedged round with clichés and unexamined assumptions.

Received clichés

Four of these clichés will be addressed at the beginning of the book. The first is that the written text is a 'blueprint' for performance and therefore 'incomplete' until so realised. The second is that theatre/drama is a 'collaborative' art. The third is that writing drama is a 'visual' art. Fourth, the dramatic text is commonly characterised as either difficult to read, or simply unreadable in its so-called incomplete written form. Only through performance, goes the argument, can it be really understood and, in that hermeneutic sense, 'read'. At the level of common sense, each of these has its resonances; but I think it is vital to begin by deconstructing them all, in order to clear a space for proper attention to the art of writing drama.

During the decades in which I've taught playwriting much has changed. The Creative Writing landscape has been transformed, with under- and postgraduate degree courses proliferating. Along with developing my own method of teaching the art of writing drama, I have also gained extensive experience in teaching poetry and prose fiction writing at university level and in adult education. As a result of this, I am certain that one of the most important elements in understanding the practice of the art of writing drama is to know what makes it distinctive from other imaginative forms, particularly prose fiction.

This book will, I hope, be of interest and use to many different groups of people. Drama-writing courses in adult education can be augmented by encouraging students to think about what they are doing, while they develop their drama-writing skills. Those involved in devising, in dramaturgy, directors and producers interested in generating dramatic writing will, I hope, understand more about the difficult and discrete practices in which the dramatist (student and professional) engages. In higher education the imperative to think about, theorise, as well as engage in the practice of learning by doing is powerful.

The book will be of use to teachers of creative writing, enabling them to expand courses they already teach, or are developing. It will also be useful to students who are interested in the relationship between writing drama as practice, and the excitements of conceptualisation involved in reading and understanding cultural theory. The book will help to bring a practical application into Theatre and Performance Studies, and perhaps contribute to bridging the gap across increasing specialisation at academic and professional levels. Above all, it will contribute to the understanding of anyone who is interested in what is involved in the art of writing drama.

This book makes an unabashed call for the rehabilitation of the dramatist as writer and of the dramatic text as a distinctive form of writing. I believe that by so doing, a space is created to bridge the pedagogic and vocational, and to help clarify the relationship between writing and performance, from the perspective of the dramatist.

1 Drama – the apparently incomplete text

There is, wrote Raymond Williams, a 'confusion, both theoretical and practical, in our contemporary understanding of the relation between a dramatic text and a dramatic performance . . .'[1] This 'confusion', or question, is at the heart of writing drama.

There are a number of terms used for the dramatic (written) text: 'blueprint' is perhaps the most common, but there are others. Playwright Ronald Hayman described it as 'more like a code or a musical score, as a scenario for a series of theatrical impacts which can be achieved only in a public performance'.[2] Director David Jones commented that: 'a play is a stepping stone to the theatrical event which is the play in performance.'[3] Sam Smily defined further: 'A written play, by itself, isn't a completed work of art, but an important ingredient for the creation of drama.'[4] Jean-Claude van Italie advised: 'Don't think of a script as an end in itself, but as a musical score for actors' voices and a blueprint for theatrical action.'[5] Playwright and director Alan Ayckbourn wrote that for him, 'writing . . . is in a sense only the preparatory notes for the

---

[1] *Drama in Performance* (Penguin, 1972), p. 4. First published in 1968.
[2] *How to Read a Play* (Grove Press, 1977), p. 9.
[3] *Making Plays*, Richard Nelson and David Jones, ed. Colin Chambers (Faber, 1995), p. 58.
[4] *Playwriting*, by Sam Smily (with Norman A. Bert), (Yale University Press, 2005), p. 10. First published by Prentice Hall, 1971
[5] *The Playwright's Workbook* (Applause, 1997), p. 17.

directing process; directing is the continuation and completion of the writing.'[6]

Some of these pronouncements derive from the work of academics, distinguishing between different parts of the theatrical process, some from teachers and writers of drama, attempting to formulate an aesthetics of dramatic writing. Ayckbourn, of course, wrote as both writer and director, with the above quote coming from the point of view of the director in him. Similar comments are often made about writing for film. Robert McKee, in his lucid and influential book on writing for the silver screen, commented, 'A literary work is finished and complete within itself. A screenplay waits for the camera.'[7]

Clearly, there are both theoretical and practical reasons for this assertion of the putative 'incompleteness' of the drama-writing process. But whatever the reasons, historical, academic or industrial, the idea that a dramatic script is 'incomplete' amounts to a deeply problematic cliché. I am deliberately calling it a cliché because it has become an unthinking way to undermine the importance of the dramatic text and therefore of the dramatist's work. By virtue of constant assertion, the cliché is elevated to quasi-theoretical status, or to a 'universal' truth.

From the notion that the written dramatic text is 'incomplete' follow a number of assumptions. Especially significant is the implication that the text does not exist adequately as an object for scrutiny until it has been lifted off the page and embodied in performance. It must, therefore, be difficult to read and understand: 'It is because the playtext is such a strange – incomplete – object – that it seems useful to have a guide as to how someone might get the most out of dealing with this object.'[8]

The idea that the dramatist produces an incomplete text puts him/her into a strange situation. She/he supposedly produces

---

[6] *The Crafty Art of Playmaking* (Faber, 2003), p. ix.

[7] *Story* (Methuen, 1999), p. 394.

[8] *Studying Plays* by S. Shepherd and M. Wallis (Edward Arnold, 1998), p. 1.

something inherently secondary, always lesser and offering only a starting point, a signpost for the 'real thing', for which the director and the rest of the team are responsible, because (a) performance is considered more important than text-on-the page, because (b) it is only in performance that 'real' meaning is created. This is a profoundly ironic state of affairs, given that Theatre Studies still direct considerable serious attention to playwrights and plays, and that (word-free theatre apart) there can be no performance and therefore no theatre without written texts. One might at this point legitimately wonder why any writer should ever bother to sit down and write something which is inherently incomplete. Because they're star struck, plain masochistic, or humbly grateful that they are being allowed to experience some of the glamour and excitement attached to performance?

Drama as collaborative art

The second, and related, cliché, is that theatre/film etc. are 'collaborative' arts. This, too, demands further examination. In all dramatic forms of production there are clearly demarcated skills – a division of labour: who does what and the ways in which different skills and functions link and combine in the finished performance. This product appears seamless, but is clearly the result of a long list of skills which contribute to the finished artefact. The person with whom the dramatist has his/her main working relationship is the director. In this relationship there is a clear division of labour: the writer writes, the director directs. Sounds simple. The writer has the skill to do one thing well, the director has the skill to do another thing well. Each refines his/her expertise during the course of his/her cultural practice as part of the production of the dramatic event in performance.

However, director and writer occupy different positions of temporal authority, or power, within the production process. These are not just straightforward distinctions of artistic skill. Whereas the writer's job begins and ends with the act of producing the written text (writers may be consulted on casting, set etc., but even when consultation is enshrined in a contract, it doesn't guarantee full consultation, participation or agreement), the director's responsibility extends over a far wider field.

The director is the person responsible for co-ordinating all the artistic and technical skills, including the contribution of the writer. Ultimately, the director is accountable to the management/ producer. This gives the director overarching responsibility and an inevitable degree of power, and this is the predominant working model which operates in all the performance industries.

Put bluntly, the dramatist is completely dependent on his/her director. A dramatic text will stand or fall on its first showing/ production, depending on the director's achievement. Good direction and performance (begging the detailed question of what that is!) can cover weaknesses in the writing. Bad direction (ditto) can destroy a brilliant text. Inadequate or uneven direction might blur or leave under-realised aspects of the written text.

Directors, particularly artistic directors of theatres and companies, have the commissioning power upon which all dramatists depend for professional survival, publication of their texts and the ability to make a living. Dramatists survive, and enjoy the opportunity to develop their work, if their plays continue to be produced and, for this to happen, the plays must also be published. Only a relatively small number of new plays reach publication and these tend to come from the larger, more prestigious theatres, and only if the first production is successful.

When a dramatic text in any medium goes into production, however welcome the writer may be, whatever changes might be made to the text during the process, the writer's job is essentially done. The writer becomes an informed spectator, but nevertheless no more than that: a spectator with special interests, but not a central participant. The director is in a position to influence the script, but the dramatist is, very largely indeed, very unlikely ever to be in a position to exert much influence over a production. At best, his/her responses and comments all filter through to the director, who is (must be) the final decision maker.

Production can as easily (some might say more easily) take place without the writer as with him/her present. During the 1970s the Writers' Guild and the Theatre Writers' Union spent a great deal of time putting in place a contract, which asserted and protected theatre writers' rights. The right to presence in rehearsal was a hard-won principle – and one for which the writer is paid only a very small token amount. BBC radio drama contracts have a participation clause with a pitifully tiny payment for a day's attendance. In film, the writer has an even tougher time. This is not likely to encourage any writer to believe his/her presence in rehearsal (or, indeed, their work perhaps) is really taken seriously or fully acknowledged.

Writing drama as an imaginative mode of thought

These comments do not derive from a conviction that the dramatist is a hermetic, arrogant creature, superior to all other interaction with fellow dramatic workers. Nor is it to suggest that the dramatist 'should', as of right, be a full participant during the rehearsal process. Many aspiring dramatists gain an enormous amount from working with directors on rehearsed readings, or the first productions of their plays. It is often the case that new plays are subject to some form of rewriting during rehearsal. This is not a bad thing, as long as the director is not peremptory. Often the revelations that follow from the excitement and insights of rehearsal contribute to producing more finished writing, and enable the dramatist to continue writing in the future with greater understanding and skill. The point I want to make here is that, in general, if the fundamental, conceptual work has not been done by the dramatist *before* a written text seriously enters the production process (i.e., the director's first reading and then rehearsal), no amount of tinkering stands much significant chance of transforming the work. Writing takes a long time; it entails thinking, imagining, thinking, writing and thinking and rewriting. A great deal – if not all – of this takes place away from the rehearsal floor. All dramatists know this.

Dramatic writing, as such, is therefore not intrinsically a collaborative art form, any more than writing novels or poetry is collaborative. Clearly, there is teamwork involved later in the process and because part of the team (in the form of the cast) is visible onstage and their names are listed in the programme (or film credits), it may appear as though in some way they have all consciously worked as a collaborative team.

In the performance arts, many people with different skills work together on the same production, but they do not all have the same decision-making power, or the same creative options. Indeed, none of these people can begin work properly until they have something to start work on and with. The dramatist's resources and raw materials come from different sources or origins, closer to those of writers of other imaginative literary forms.

Writing drama is a matter of entering a particular mode of imaginative thought, which is then realised in terms of a particular set of writerly (literary, if you like) conventions. For this reason there is no automatic cause-and-effect relationship between writing and performance: a drama is not written 'for' performance, even though performance is one of its possible forms (and, in many cases, the only one) of publication.

Real teamwork, democratic or otherwise, only fully happens when it is structured in such a way that everyone both contributes her/his own skill, while acknowledging the other skills within the relevant existing power structure. This can be very strictly hierarchical, or with different kinds of inbuilt egalitarianism. The experiences can be productive and, equally, they may be frustrating and oppressive. It all depends, in the end, on the working ethos and, in the most conventional working structures, on the relationship between writer and director. The cosy idea that it is just all, in some way, 'collaborative', serves to mask the authority structure, keep the writer in a constrained place and conceal the extraordinary and distinctive imaginative process with which a dramatist works.

Drama as a visual medium

As an extension of the notion of the written text as only one component of a collaborative art comes the concomitant cliché that writing drama is a 'visual' art. This, too, needs to be unpacked. Of course, all dramatic texts have a very powerful relationship to the 'visual', insofar as performance is seen and heard, and is literally visualised by its other participants. In terms of the text itself, the concept of the 'visual' is considered to be contained within the device of 'stage directions', or information which relates mostly to what is 'seen' in performance, rather than what is heard – i.e., the dialogue. However, at best, stage directions are ambiguous and unstable elements in drama, and need discussion in their own right (see chapter 8).

Misunderstandings about stage directions come about because of an inadequate grasp of how a dramatist works and what she/he does, and also because of a fundamental theoretical confusion about the written text itself and the ways in which it relates to, and is distinct from, prose fiction. The particular dominance of dialogue, or the utterance, or speech acts in dramatic fiction demand attention, and will be discussed in more detail later in this book (see chapter 9). But dialogue is primarily aural rather than visual, even though in performance it is an element in what is 'seen'. Dialogue is embodied (voiced) by the performer, not made visual. If that were so, radio drama would be an impossibility. In radio, everything is heard and not seen.

Drama as the novel manqué

The final cliché, that the dramatic text is either hard to read or unreadable, has two related implications. First is the more obvious assumption that, because it is 'incomplete', subject to completion in production/performance, it can only be partially read by the lay person (and then only with difficulty), or read by the expert (i.e., the director/producer), who will then become the Svengali to bring together all the component parts in performance. Second is a more profound, hermeneutical implication: if the dramatic text cannot be properly 'read' on the page, this suggests that its meanings, or any meanings it may have, or convey, or contain, or yield, are either inaccessible or only partially accessible on the page, and (to complete the familiar circular argument) only finally 'meaningful' in and via performance. This is particularly ironic in view of how much time is still spent studying, analysing and writing about the dramatic text on the page, and how many academic books and articles address drama on the page as a distinctive kind of literary text (which, of course, it is).

If the dramatic text is unreadable, or only readable with difficulty, the implication is that it can only be 'read' with special training – something beyond the ability of most readers. While this expressed 'difficulty' must be taken seriously, it must also be seen in its proper context. The notion owes far less to any supposed 'difficulty' of reading the dramatic text than to the fact that in our culture the novel is still the dominant fictional form, providing a reading 'norm'. This means that anyone deciding to read a dramatic text comes to it with conscious, or unconscious, expectations of what she/he may find, by implicitly comparing it to the experience of reading prose fiction.

Within the convention of the novel, some kind of overarching narrative voice generally sets the terms of reading. Without this, and the conventional elements of paragraphs of 'description', details about the thoughts and feelings (the so-called 'inner life') of the characters, back story, etc., the dramatic text may appear to some people to be lacking, to be relatively empty, to be, in a sense, full of gaps. Put together with the assumption that only performance yields significant meaning, the 'gaps' seem to be insurmountable, or, at best, suspended in favour of a different event: the related, but very different, artefact of performance. The overarching importance of dialogue (even in the film script) is replaced in the novel by swathes of prose. Dialogue in the novel is generally a minor element. Yet again, then, in relation to the dominant literary convention the dramatic text becomes an 'incomplete' piece of fiction (i.e., composed of 'minor' elements) with the important bits missing. Dialogue remains in its misconceived place as lesser, secondary, unfamiliar.

Conclusions

Altogether, then, ideas about the incomplete text, seeing the written work as only one element in a collaborative process, the privileging of the physical/visual over the written and the assumptions about hermeneutical partiality as applied to the dramatic text do not exactly combine to shape an identifiable object which the dramatist produces – and which can be subject to some kind of literary autonomy and, therefore, susceptible to productive pedagogic treatment, let alone performance.

Ironically, while the published, performed and/or canonical (live or dead) dramatist is privileged, as a working writer she/he is theoretically diminished. The provenance of the writer's professional practice is represented as incomplete, partial, secondary, relatively unimportant. The Death of the Author is far more than a sophisticated postmodern conceit; the phrase encapsulates with painful poignancy the way dramatists and the dramatic text are generally approached, both by the cultural industries and in many of today's most influential forms of academic theatre studies.

Performance, reception theory and semiology, different ways of understanding the signifying process of dramatic production, developed in part as a reaction against the historical convention of studying plays-on-the-page. This academic over-compensation has helped construct a tacit definition of the role of the dramatist as someone who necessarily writes an incomplete text.

Performance theory, interesting and important as it always is, is also inherently unstable and provisional, especially in relation to theatre. No one performance is ever absolutely identical to any other, and each production is necessarily distinctive and unrepeatable. There is never a fixed performance 'object', which can be reliably identified – compared, for example, to a book, although here too there will be different editions of texts, sometimes with changes incorporated. This is borne out by academic attitudes to writing drama. As Susan Bennett pointed out in writing about audience-reception theory, 'The usefulness of a discourse which took account of receptive processes was undercut by its neglect of the dramatic text and performance.'[9]

The analytically useful distinctions between 'dramatic text' and 'performance text' have led to new forms of study, analysis and understanding of the ways in which meaning is created in performance. An understanding of performance theory as well as the conditions of performance can only benefit the student of writing drama, but solely in the context of a reconceived idea of what the dramatist does and in what the dramatic text consists.

The compleat dramatist

The idea that the dramatist is entirely responsible for the complete dramatic text is not a return to outdated concepts and assumptions.

[9] *Theatre Audiences* (Routledge, 2003), p. 20. First published 1997.

It is not an argument for just studying the play-on-the-page, or just seeing a drama as a quirky kind of novel manqué. In any case, a book about the art of writing drama must take account of the performance-related aspects of dramatic writing, while not allowing them to usurp writerly considerations.

But the argument that the dramatist produces a complete text these days seem to be an oddly radical-seeming challenge to the way in which both text and dramatist now largely carry an extended 'minority' status, with the dramatist marginalised. To reclaim the primacy of the written text for the dramatist is by no means too extreme a point of view. It is not an ideological battle for who controls the 'meaning' of the text (dramatic or performance), but rather a new and complex acknowledgement of the dramatist's responsibility and a refusal to allow the performance industries or Performance Studies to colonise the power of the text for their own purposes.

The idea that the dramatic text is secondary has provoked pockets of resistance. Appeals for the rehabilitation of dramatist and text have come from different quarters, not merely, as might be expected, from dramatists themselves. During the 1970s playwright John Arden argued for an 'eventual aim of re-establishing the Playwright in a useful and fulfilling role'.[10] While himself part of the movement to politicise theatre, nevertheless he saw the dangers of attributing accusations of manipulation in the theatre to the 'tyranny' of the text: 'the idea is allowed to evolve that the only way to save the theatre from its moribund state is to down-grade the script and to concentrate entirely upon the "vital" values of performance.'[11]

Looking back from the perspective of contemporary literary and cultural theory, Elinor Fuchs commented on the 1960s generation: 'Never before . . . had the dramatic text been looked on as the enemy, rather than the vehicle, of theatrical presentations . . . many

[10] *To Present the Pretence* (Eyre Methuen, 1977), p. 179.
[11] Ibid., p. 188.

theatres came to regard the author's script as an element of political oppression in the theatrical process . . .'[12] For her, precisely as the result of the greater understanding afforded to performance, 'The text comes out from the wings as a separated theatrical element . . .'[13]

There is a dialectically more complex and accurate way of understanding the relation between the dramatic text and dramatic performance, which is concealed when the same word – 'text' – is applied to each. While a 'text' in its postmodern connotations clearly refers to an object to which an identifiable system of literary signification can be applied, it has conspired to blur what is otherwise a clear point of departure for dramatic writing and to imply a competition between different 'texts' for primacy. It is, of course, a competition for authorship – particularly of meaning; as if the academic could usurp the worldly attribution of authorship to the individual dramatist.

In fact, of course, the text never went away, just as the conceit of the Death of the Author never abolished either authorship or textual responsibility. The power and importance of postmodern theories still dominate academic study and are still being worked through. However, even during the period in which they developed, there were other ideological positions.

An incisive comment from Terry Eagleton returns us neatly to a way of approaching the relative autonomy of the dramatic text and of the dramatist's role: 'A dramatic performance is clearly more than a "reflection" of the dramatic text; on the contrary . . . it is a transformation of the text into a unique product, which involves reworking it in accordance with the specific demands and conditions of theatrical performance . . . what has intervened . . . is a trans-formative labour.'[14]

This approach seeks to establish the ways in which the dramatic and performance 'texts' can coexist and still retain autonomy. This

[12] *The Death of Character* (Indiana University Press, 1996), p. 70.
[13] Ibid., p. 91.
[14] *Marxism and Literary Criticism* (Methuen, 1976), p. 51.

can enable us to plot the relationship *between* texts, and produces a synthesis between the contradictory historic argument that an understanding of performance is secondary to the written text and the postmodern attempt to reduce the written text to what is virtually a by-product of performance. It is on this basis that a realistic prospect of teaching the art of writing drama becomes possible.

2 The emergence of the dramatist and drama in education

While writing drama may be a relative latecomer to today's academic creative writing boom, it had an important role to play in the history of Creative Writing (CW) in America. When English literature was first established as a university subject at the end of the nineteenth century, studies of Composition in the English language accompanied it. In the US, writing instruction is still compulsory for first-year American college students.

D. G. Myers, the main historian of CW in the US, has summarised the trajectory of its development:

> The story of creative writing began with the opposition to philology and resumes with the effort in the 1880s and 1890s to restore literary and educational value to the teaching of rhetoric . . . English composition was the first widely successful attempt to offer instruction in writing in English . . . it was formulated at Harvard in the last quarter of the century out of a constructivist belief that the ideal end of the study of literature is the making of literature . . . English composition established the autonomy of college writing and created a demand for courses in writing from a literary and constructivist point of view. And these were necessary preconditions of creative writing's acceptance as a subject of serious study . . . Until about the 1920s, though, there was small need for creative writing per

se because English composition and creative writing were one and the same thing.'[1]

It is interesting that, in some pioneering universities, playwriting was an important presence even at this early stage. At Harvard, George Pierce Baker set up an advanced course called 'The Technique of the Drama' in 1906. He had taught a similar course the previous year at Radcliffe, a women-only college. In 1919 he published *Dramatic Technique*, based on a series of lectures originally delivered in 1913.[2] He claimed that learning to write drama constituted a valid university subject in its own right and demanded its own pedagogic approaches. The fact that it 'has had for centuries in England and elsewhere a fecund history before the novel took shape at all would intimate that the drama is a different and independent art from that of the novel and short story'.[3] Baker was not the only pioneer. The Carnegie Institute of Technology set up an undergraduate drama programme in 1914 and the first graduate programme was started at Yale in 1926.

When English literature was established in British universities, also across the end of the nineteenth and the beginning of the twentieth centuries, there was one very important difference: the study of composition did not become a part of its curricular development. This meant that the principle of writing instruction has never been an intrinsic part of university English Studies in the UK, and for this reason (and other culture-specific ones) creative writing arrived much later in higher education in this country – indeed, formally not until after World War Two. Nevertheless, on both sides of the Atlantic the revival of professional high-art theatre at the end of the nineteenth century proved significant.

The emergence of the fully professional writer in the UK dates from this time, covering different genres – journalism, scholarship,

---

[1] *The Elephants Teach* (Prentice-Hall, 1996), p. 36–37.
[2] Da Capo, 1976.
[3] Ibid., p. 5.

the novel, poetry and drama. In a passionate, campaigning book, *The Pen and the Book*,[4] published in 1899, Walter Besant warned professional writers against the rapacious demands of publishers, defended the respectability of the professional writer, provided down-to-earth advice about contracts, described the difficulty of the 'Literary Life', and outlined the differences between writing poetry, prose fiction and drama. Aware of the 'great increase in the number of theatres' in London,[5] he predicted, indeed, that the drama would take over from the novel: 'In fifty years' time the English imagination will, perhaps, assume instinctively a dramatic form, as it now assumes the form of fiction: there will be two or three hundred theatres in London and its suburbs.'[6]

Besant, one of the founders of the Society of Authors in the 1880s, himself wrote in all genres. William Archer, on the other hand, while not himself a dramatist, confirmed a demand for textbooks 'on the art and craft of drama . . . It is not so with the novel. Popular as is that form of literature, guides to novel-writing, if they exist at all, are comparatively rare.'[7] Archer was a theatre reviewer and translator, and was instrumental in helping to bring Ibsen's plays to the London stage.

Besant's and Archer's books accompanied a wave of socially aware new drama, strongly influenced by European companies, many of which visited London: 'The eighteen-nineties witnessed the emergence of independent theatre movements in a number of European cities. Antoine's Théâtre Libre in Paris, the Freie Bühne in Berlin, the Independent Theatre in London, the Abbey in Dublin, the Moscow Art Theatre, proclaimed a new faith in the drama's integrity and social function.'[8]

[4] Thomas Burleigh, 1899.

[5] Ibid., p. 107.

[6] Ibid., p. 114.

[7] *Play-making: a manual of craftsmanship* (Dodo Press reprint, originally published 1912), p. 1.

[8] *Theory and Technique of Playwriting* by John Howard Lawson (Putnam's, 1949), p. 83.

Antoine's 'Théâtre Libre' was a subscription society, founded in 1887 for new drama; the Moscow Art Theatre was founded in 1898, notably producing the plays of Anton Chekhov. As a result of visits from these companies during the 1880s and 1890s, J. T. Grein founded the Independent Theatre Society, in London in 1891. This was a subscription society, 'giving occasional performances of serious new drama, unhampered by the constraints of official censorship and commercial accountability.'[9] They put on the first English production of Ibsen's *Ghosts* in 1891 and presented plays by George Bernard Shaw: 'The Independent Theatre produced twenty-eight plays in seven years, and together with the Stage Society, which succeeded it in 1899, was responsible for establishing what Matthew Arnold called an "ethical drama" . . .'[10] Renewed interest in reviving the theatre of the past accompanied these developments: actor-manager William Poel set up the Elizabethan Stage Society in 1894, 'for the purpose of presenting Shakespeare uncut, without scene changes, and on stages corresponding to the Tudor originals'.[11]

These entrepreneurial moves generated a rapid increase in new drama and in the emergence, not only of the dramatist as a distinct and (sometimes) respected professional, but also of the modern director. As Edward Braun has pointed out, even before this time, someone always had overall responsibility for the 'production'. In Shakespeare's time it might have been the dramatist, later it was actor-playwrights such as Molière, or actor-managers such as Garrick and Poel. Constantin Stanislavsky 'became Russia's first stage-director in the true sense of the word', in 1890.[12] In the English theatre, Harley Granville-Barker, who was also a playwright, staged plays by Ibsen in the early years of the twentieth century, encouraging indigenous new work. By this time

[9] *The Director and the Stage* by Edward Braun (Methuen, 1983), p. 77.
[10] Ibid., pp. 77–8.
[11] Ibid.
[12] Ibid., p. 60.

playwrights such as John Galsworthy, John Masefield and George Bernard Shaw were becoming, according to Braun, box-office attractions in their own right.

Besant and Archer recognised that this new interest in theatre constituted an important cultural force. Enthusiasm was high: 'In the forty years leading up to the outbreak of the First World War the English theatre reached a new level of popularity and commercial success. Between 1880 and 1900 fourteen new theatres opened in London alone, and many existing ones were completely renovated. With their extravagantly gilded and plush upholstered interiors and with the previously uncomfortable pit benches replaced by high-priced orchestra stalls, a night at the theatre acquired a new decorum and sense of occasion, which precisely matched the opulent respectability of the affluent middle-class of Victorian England.'[13]

Drama and education

The idea that drama could be a means to an end accompanied the incorporation of English literature into schools and adult education. The adult education movement has been of great importance in this country; during most of the nineteenth century English literature was more widely taught in classes run by the University Extension Movement than it was at universities. Even before Oxford and Cambridge formally adopted English as part of their degree courses, these popular tutorial classes were being extensively taught by campaigners for the 'subject' to be accepted at universities. In this context Shakespeare's plays had a dual function: as a study of poetry on the page, and as part of the practical, authenticist revival of theatre production undertaken by Poel and others.

In 1921 the Board of Education set up an Adult Education

---

[13] Ibid., p. 77.

Committee and commissioned a report on *The Drama in Adult Education* (1926). The committee, which included a number of enthusiastic amateur theatre practitioners, as well as Harley Granville-Barker, identified drama as 'an instrument of education'.[14]

This was also an important element in the early twentieth-century Progressive School movement, in both the US and the UK. Indeed, Myers has argued that creative writing as such was first taught in American schools in the 1920s, before it joined Composition as a university subject. In the UK there were a small number of progressive schools, such as Bedales, Dartington and Summerhill, based on radical, co-educational, child-centred approaches to education. They were concerned to send their pupils into the world as independent and responsible citizens. As part of this philosophy, all the arts were seen as important and included in the curriculum. There was a particularly prominent role for music, speech and drama. Pupils wrote the plays, made costumes and sets, and performed. While the writing component was, of course, important, it was only one element in encouraging group- and teamwork, and diverse forms of co-operation and collaboration.

More explicitly writing-centred approaches were fostered by two figures. H. Caldwell Cook, teacher at the boys' Perse School in Cambridge (where the influential critics F. R. Leavis and E. M. W. Tillyard went to school) published a book called *The Play-Way* in 1917,[15] where he encouraged his boy pupils to write poetry and stories, as well as drama. Some decades later Marjorie Hourd published *The Education of the Poetic Spirit*[16] in 1949. Her work, with girls from eight or nine upwards, involved using *The Iliad*, the legends of King Arthur and Shakespeare's plays as a basis for the children's own dramatic writing. This was partly to develop the

[14] *Drama/Theatre/Performance* by Simon Shepherd and Mick Wallis (Routledge, 2004), p. 12.
[15] Heinemann.
[16] Heinemann, 1962

children's original creativity, but also, very consciously, as a way to foster and encourage a greater understanding of the literature they were reading by *doing*, by exploring the forms through their own writing.

Using drama in this way, as a means to an educational end, has now become pretty well taken for granted. The most recent professional manifestation of this is Theatre in Education (TIE), developed in the 1960s, with groups attached to professional theatres as a form of educational outreach. Often the presentations are group devised, sometimes by professionals who take productions into schools, sometimes creating productions together with pupils. Clearly, with such specific target audiences and a focused educational purpose, the subject matter and treatment are tailored to fit, as it were. Here writing and performance are at the service of the context and the desired issue-based aims, with benefits for teachers and pupils.

The idea that 'doing' drama can also function as a 'learning medium'[17] expands the horizons of the 'collaborative' idea discussed in the previous chapter. In this context the processes of making drama, dictated by the imperatives of performance and working in and with groups, rather than the individually centred process of writing as such, are foregrounded. The notion that this kind of teamwork can be socially beneficial to individuals, groups and ultimately the wider society is powerful. Drama has also become an important element in therapeutic processes; in social rehabilitation and, interestingly, in corporate management training – where role-play exercises provide an imaginative insight into certain kinds of formal interactive relationships at work.

In their potential for uses in a wide variety of contexts, with very different groups of people, the aims of these 'dramas' and the organisation, structure and control of the processes are likely to

[17] *Dorothy Heathcote: Drama as a Learning Medium* by Betty Jane Wagner (Hutchinson, 1985). First published in the US in 1976.

vary. In such applied uses of drama the interaction, or interface, between the 'art' – the invention of relevant situations, role play ('pretending' to be someone else) – are tightly tailored to the particular constituency and situation.

Teaching drama after World War Two

In the UK the next pioneering educational stage for drama was the establishment of discrete drama departments, separate from English. The first was set up after the Second World War at Bristol University in 1947, to study the history of theatre and drama. Initially, the approach was still strongly shaped by a focus similar to that on the literary text in English departments. The importance of performance was acknowledged but at that point drama as a university subject 'was in tension both with the textual analysis that was then fashionable in English departments and with the training done in acting schools'.[18]

This led to a rather interesting division of labour. While university drama courses focused largely on the play-on-the-page, and on the history of performance, undergraduates often took charge of performance and production. At Oxford and Cambridge, university-wide and college-based drama groups produced plays throughout the academic year. At Cambridge, for example, where I was a student in the early 1960s, plays staged by the undergraduates were far more up to date and avant-garde than any of the drama texts on the syllabus.

Although I was not particularly conscious of it at the time, some of my fellow undergraduates were already aware of contemporary drama hot from its first professional production. Some of the new playwrights visited these university productions and in this way many students who later became professional performers and

[18] Shepherd and Wallis, op. cit., p. 40.

directors created their own autodidactic environment for exploring contemporary drama. Many graduates went into theatre, BBC radio drama, TV and film, becoming producers, directors and performers. There was thus a direct line into the professional theatre from these universities. Very few of them wrote plays as students. It was not until the later 1960s, influenced by the turbulent political and cultural climate, that undergraduate generations began writing plays, continuing to do so in the rapidly expanding alternative theatre world after the end of censorship in 1968.

After censorship, new dramatists and new drama

At the Royal Court Theatre, John Osborne's *Look Back in Anger* (1956) symbolised the arrival of a new generation of playwrights, initiating what has become our canon of contemporary drama. Even under official censorship the British theatre of the 1950s had begun to introduce different content and experiences onto the stage, drawing on popular forms of theatre, as well as the legacy of the well-made naturalistic play, which dated from earlier in the twentieth century. Joan Littlewood at the Theatre Royal in London's Stratford East, for example, along with directors in regional theatres, began to stage plays about ordinary people, in contrast to the middle- and upper-class drawing-room theatre of London's commercial West End. Theatre historian John Elsom observed, 'Within ten years suave actors had been replaced by rough ones as heroes, metropolitan accents by regional ones, stylish decadents by frustrated "working-class" heroes.'[19]

As the 1960s progressed, this theatre generated increasing pressure on the government to repeal the censorship laws. Socialism, feminism, the gay movement, avant-garde artistic experiments in

[19] *Post-War British Theatre* (Routledge, 1979), p. 34.

poetry, performance art and theatre, all infused the theatre with ways of democratising theatre-making and theatre-going. As Susan Bennett commented, 'Since the 1960s many theatres have emerged which speak for dominated and generally marginalised peoples . . .'[20] Influenced by a politics which began to contest social, gender and racial cultural biases, this theatre drew new attention to the numbers of women and members of minority ethnic groups who were or were not contributing to the variety and richness of the theatre world.

The heightened political awareness of the time helped to draw attention to the maverick and freelance insecurity of dramatists themselves. In 1977 a group of playwrights (of whom I was one) founded the Theatre Writers' Union (TWU) which, for the first time, negotiated standard agreements between dramatists and West End, repertory and small theatres. These agreements are still in place, supported by the two main unions which represent writers: the Writers' Guild and the Society of Authors. Walter Besant's warnings about the need to protect theatre writers finally found fulfilment, nearly a century later.

The dramatists who emerged from the alternative theatre movement joined those who were being actively encouraged by directors of theatres devoted to producing new plays. Theatre history, studied through the lasting reputations of produced and published playwrights, sometimes gives the impression that the dramatists 'lead' the production process. In fact, it has always been the case that new writing in the theatre comes about because of the insights and adventurous decisions made by the artistic directors of theatres. Of course, these people are responding to what dramatists are writing, or want to write, but such drama is only staged if those who run theatres are willing to take the risks. Writers – with the honourable and probably unique exception of Alan Ayckbourn – are very rarely in such executive decision-making positions. The pioneers of our vital modern theatre were artistic directors such as

[20] *Theatre Audiences*, p. 1.

George Devine and Joan Littlewood who, at the Royal Court theatre and at the Theatre Royal, Stratford East respectively, were highly influential in encouraging new writing. After censorship ended many theatres made sure they had a smaller studio theatre attached to the main house, with the express purpose of putting on new writing.

3 The performance text

The academic counterpart to the radical theatres of the 1970s was the development of Performance Studies. Influenced by revived intellectual interest in continental theory and post-Marxist writing, Performance Studies expanded the sources and possibilities for conceptualising the way meaning was/is created in theatre. Drawing on developments in semiology, this was a valuable addition to the established academic convention of only studying plays-on-the-page.[1]

Theory

One of the most vital, if sometimes intractable, questions about what theatre 'is' was formulated by Raymond Williams as the 'relation between a dramatic text and a dramatic performance'.[2] The concept of performance rightly directs attention to the 'realised' dramatic event and thus, by implication, also to the audience/spectators. However, in the theorised attempts to understand the role of the audience as creators of 'meaning', a three-way tension is created between the written text, the realised performance and the

---

[1] See, for example, *The Semiotics of Theatre and Drama* by Keir Elam (Routledge, 1997). Originally published in 1980.
[2] *Drama in Performance* by Raymond Williams (Penguin, 1972), p. 2.

audience. This can easily become a contested way of trying to determine in an absolute way exactly where 'meaning' is significantly created, as well as how.

If this is seen as a singular, monolithic question – i.e., the idea that meaning is created *either* in the written text, *or* in performance, *or* by the audience – we are in danger of reducing serious conceptual and practical discussion to a matter of competition, with the remaining two elements somehow seen as secondary, or neutral, or as creating not-meaning. If that is what we do, then we must add other meaning-creating figures to those jostling for interpretive supremacy: the critic, who reviews performance, and, later, the academic, who may study any or all of these, or any permutation of them, as well as those who study the play on the page as a literary text. The truth is that meanings are inevitably created at every stage along the way of writing/producing/performing/publishing drama. Drama theory becomes particularly difficult, because its real task should be to clarify the relationship between these different moments of meaning-creation.

In the sometimes abstruse field of literary and cultural theory, Valentine Cunningham has cut to the chase, returning us usefully to some basic principles. In one of the most eruditely sceptical and exhilarating books produced in the wake of literary theory, *Reading After Theory*, he commented:

> Certainly everything that Theory comprises, operates on one zone or another, or in some combination, of what have proved the main continuing focuses of literary theory since poetics and discussion of aesthetics began with the Greeks and Romans. There's only ever been up for grabs, for theory, a simple trio of knowable, thinkable, zones, corresponding to the three components of the basic model of linguistic communication. There is always, and only ever, a sender, a message, and a received – a writer, a text, a reader – the act of writing, the thing written, the reading of the written thing – the literary input, the

> literary object found to be 'there', reader(s) attending to this thereness. Or, if you like, cause, consequence, effect. Only three: but a mighty three for all that. And the whole history of criticism, of theorising, is merely a history of the varying, shifting preoccupation across the ages with these three zones, and with these three alone.'[3]

Of course, when we take this triumvirate and relate it to performance, each category is compounded. The 'sender' consists of the written text plus all those working on the production. The 'message' is divided between performance, production and published written text (or filmed/recorded event). The 'reader' also becomes multiple; not just because of the pluralist presence of the audience(s) at the moment of the consumption of performance, but also because any written text has already been subject to various kinds of 'reading' via those who have applied their transformative labour to create the performance/production. There is a parallel with reader-response theory, which argues that it is the reader of fiction who is the real creator of meaning and thus, like the audience, 'productive' of meaning. However, the vast majority of audiences for drama cannot be easily identified as individuals, or as coherent groups, for the purpose of attributing clear sources for the 'creation' of particular meanings. The use of audience questionnaires can only catch a response at one particular moment (generally, as soon as the audience has seen the drama). This cannot take into account the longer-term impact of a dramatic work, and the ways in which time and memory affect the 'meaning' it will carry for its spectator(s).

Anthropology

The theorisation of 'performance' derived its initial impetus from the disciplines and approaches of anthropology. The significant

[3] Blackwell, 2002, p. 29.

study was Erving Goffman's 1959 book, *The Presentation of Self in Everyday Life*. Here the rituals and ceremonies of everyday life were elaborated into a metaphorically articulated series of roles and performances. Goffman 'built his work on the basis that everyday life is framed and performed'.[4] Richard Schechner developed this work, relating it to theatre and comparing the assumptions of Western traditions with those from other performance cultures: 'Ritualised behaviour extends across the entire range of human action, but performance is a particular heated arena of ritual, and theatre, script and drama are heated and compact areas of performance.'[5]

The social performance rituals associated with sport, religion and theatre, for example, share certain features, particularly those defined by time and place, and the presence of an audience. A certain predetermined sequence of events takes place in designated places, at specified times. Some of the same conditions apply to other kinds of dramatic performance – film, TV, radio, video. Performance theory, when applied to theatre, demonstrates particularly clearly the insights and problems as they apply to the process of writing drama.

Schechner makes distinctions between the different elements of performance: 'To summarise thus far: the drama is what the writer writes; the script is the interior map of a particular production; the theatre is the specific set of gestures performed by the performers in any given performance; the performance is the whole event, including audience and performers (technicians, too, anyone who is there).'[6]

---

[4] *Performance Theory* by Richard Schechner (Routledge, 2003), p. 296. First published, 1977.
[5] Ibid., p. 9.
[65] Ibid., p. 87.

Performance and meaning

Performance theory, concerned as it is with meaning at a number of levels, does, however, have some baseline problems, particularly in relation to live performance: 'Theatre is . . . a live art, and its liveness poses two obstacles to study. First, it leaves us with no recallable text, no convenient and definitive reproduction we can take away and examine at leisure . . . theatre involves the simultaneous presence of both spectator and performer.'[7]

If part of the argument is that meaning is crucially created by the audience, then the nature of the entity 'audience' must also be identified and characterised, in order to be clear about the authorship of such meanings: 'The meanings offered by a particular theatrical event, then, are produced in the interaction between auditorium and stage. Theatre governs its own reading by establishing relationships, ways of viewing that enable the audience to make sense of the theatrical text . . .'[8]

However, even audience-response theorists admit to imponderable uncertainties. Both Susan Bennett and Herbert Blau, intellectually astute about performer–audience relationships, have been frank about the difficulty of defining the audience in a sufficiently precise way, in order to make it into a reliable object for analysis and study. Bennett has admitted, 'we lack any detailed picture of the theatre audience and, in particular, their role(s) in the production-reception relationship.'[9] Herbert Blau also confessed 'we simply do not know, in any reliable – no less ideal or accountable – sense, *who is there* . . . We are despite this still likely to generalise . . . about what the audience, with its disparate, cross-purposed, alienated, and incalculable perceptions, feels and felt.'[10]

This reveals a problem. On the one hand, the audience is bruited

[7] *Signs of Performance* by Colin Counsell (Routledge, 1996), p. 2.
[8] Ibid., p. 22.
[9] *Theatre Audiences*, p. 86.
[10] *The Audience* (Johns Hopkins University Press, 1990), p. 355.

as the creator of meaning and on the other it cannot be pinned down in order to elicit the meaning of any given production. There is no way, in fact, in which an audience can be appealed to for these meanings. If, at the same time, there can be no definitive material evidence of live performance which can be appealed to in support of any argument about meaning we are, seemingly, on shifting hermeneutical sands.

In the day-to-day world of performance, audience reaction is palpable and this is always taken into account by those involved in the production. If a play is designated as a comedy and no one laughs, something must be done about it. If Shakespeare's *Hamlet* produces laughs in (say) the bedroom scene between Hamlet and his mother, Gertrude, something must be done about it. The measure of applause, silence etc. – all the sounds of response from the audience – are different ways of registering the 'meanings' being communicated and/or received. But this does not make it easy to theorise, because it is a response from *that* audience to *that* moment in a production.

However, this does not mean that discussion of 'audience' in any meaningful, collective sense is impossible or irrelevant, just that one must be very careful indeed about how the term is used. It is important to distinguish between an indeterminate conception of audience, and something more specific and empirical. Creative writing pedagogy often uses the grand-sounding phrase of 'writing for an audience', as if the writer/dramatist can identify what this means on the basis of a real definition of his/her putative audience. In fact, more often than not, 'audience' is used as a posh synonym for the more down-to-earth 'market'.

Publishers and theatres do have very clear ideas about markets and audiences (the people who will spend money to buy their goods i.e., consumers), whatever 'meaning' they may derive from the 'good', once it is bought. Regional theatres, which rely heavily on local audiences, will have guidelines for what sorts of shows will fill their theatres and in these circumstances it can make some sense to think of a particular audience. But there is always the show/book, which is the exception. This is quite different from, say, the work of TIE companies who can often very clearly define the age, gender and cultural mix of their audiences, since they discuss and prepare their work together with the schools they are visiting.

Audience as political and social entity

There are circumstances where a general situation is so topical, so public and urgent, that audiences can be assumed to be bound together by their interest. For example, during the Lebanon war in the Middle East in 1983–4, three of the main Israeli theatres put on versions of Euripides' *The Trojan Women*, 'as a profound political protest against its futility and the tragic results for all involved, and particularly against the Israeli right-wing government'.[11] At the Habima Theatre the stage was designed as a huge tent, with Israeli army and Bedouin costumes to draw visual parallels. For these theatre audiences the political/artistic comparisons fed into a climate of discussion and immediate political involvement. The concept of 'audience' here operated as a synonym for certain kinds of community, sharing certain cultural and/or political contexts and concerns.

Since the end of censorship it has been possible to make topical theatre; the already much referred-to 1970s took advantage of this. During the political difficulties between the UK and Northern Ireland, events were sometimes dramatised and in recent years there have been similar docu-dramas – for example, the Frost–Nixon interviews, and various verbatim and trial plays. These only refer to an audience in the most general sense: they are plays about subjects topically in the newspapers and high up on the political agenda, and

[11] 'Theatrical Responses to Political Events', Shimon Levy and Nurit Yaari (*Journal of Theatre and Drama*, vol. 4, University of Haifa, 1998), p. 100.

the assumption is that audiences will be interested in seeing dramatic versions onstage. However, even here little more than 'interest' (i.e., enough to buy a ticket) can be assumed. There may be as many different shades of opinion in the auditorium as there are people.

Theatre and semiotics

In the area of performance theory some of the most interesting work has deployed semiology and semiotics to provide models to help understand the various elements which comprise performance. From a practical point of view these analyses are most likely to be of immediate use to directors and designers, who in any case already have very acute perceptions about cultural expectations as they relate to set design, costumes, props etc. They may not articulate these in terminologies deriving from theory, but they will know, as practitioners, that a bare stage with an orange box, which can become a table, a chair or a bed at will, will carry very different kinds of resonances from a fully furnished naturalistic 'room' with a proscenium arch to frame it. Again, it is worth stressing that this should not end up as a competition between intuition/experience and intellect.

A key initiating text in the field of semiotics and theatre area was written by Keir Elam. He applied post-Saussurian theory: 'Semiotics can best be defined as a science dedicated to the study of the production of meaning in society.'[12] When applied to theatre in particular, it is connected with 'the complex of phenomena associated with the performer-audience transaction . . .' This is distinguished from a discussion of 'drama': 'Drama, on the other hand, is meant by that mode of fiction designed for stage representation and constructed according to particular ("dramatic") conventions.'[13]

[12] Elam, op. cit., p. 1.
[13] Ibid., p. 2.

Elam tussled with the relationship between text and performance: 'This is not . . . an absolute differentiation between two mutually alien bodies, since the performance, at least traditionally, is devoted to the representation of the dramatic fiction. It demarcates, rather, different levels of a unified cultural phenomenon for purposes of analysis.'[14] It is useful to be reminded of Terry Eagleton's very clear account of how the object for semiological analysis (the performance or production) comes into being: 'A dramatic performance is clearly more than a "reflection" of the dramatic text; on the contrary . . . it is a transformation of the text into a unique product, which involves re-working it in accordance with the specific demands and conditions of theatrical performance.'[15] The practical process which links the dramatic and performance texts is encapsulated by the concept of transformative labour.

Competence and performance

The notion of prepared, theatrical performance, distinguished from the anthropologically based notion of roles 'performed' in everyday life, is returned to a parallel with ordinary life in Noam Chomsky's distinction between competence and performance: the first refers to 'the ideal general grammatical knowledge of a language possessed by a speaker of it, and "performance", the specific application of this knowledge in a speech situation'.[16] This has echoes with Saussure's notions of *langue* and *parole*, which establish a relationship between a system and specific instances of its use.

In this context, to understand anything about performance must entail an understanding of its conventions, consciously or not, theorised or not. Performance combines what is heard with what is seen; we speak and write about going to 'see' a play/performance

[14] Ibid., pp. 2–3.
[15] Eagleton, op. cit., p. 51.
[16] *Performance* by Marvin Carlson (Routledge, 2003), p. 56. First published 1996.

but, as Herbert Blau has pointed out, what we witness is through a combination of seeing and hearing: 'what we think about the relationship of the visual and the aural affects our understanding of the theatre's conventions, how we approach the stage, interpret plays, favour forms, or understand their history.'[17]

An understanding of dramatic conventions includes both the internalisation of what makes drama a distinctive written form, but also its staging/realisation. Everyone involved in creating performance, 'including playwrights, have access to shared discourses, and so can employ shared codes/logics . . . '[18] Theatre thus 'encodes meaning not merely in its overt utterances, its content, but also in its form . . .'[19]

The performance triumvirate

In terms of the specifics of performance-based creation, theatre theorists have also drawn on the work of Charles S. Peirce:

> Peirce distinguishes three kinds of sign: the *Icon*, where the sign resembles the referent, as the actor resembles a person or a stage table resembles the real thing; the *Index*, with a causal or contiguous relationship to the referent, as smoke indicates a fire, a soldier's marching stride infers his profession or a knock signifies someone on the other side of the door; the *Symbol*, where the meaning is purely conventional and relies on the agreement of all the parties involved, so that when an actor speaks the word pig we all understand that the sound refers to a particular four-legged animal . . .'[20]

[17] Blau, op. cit., p. 100.
[18] Counsell, op. cit., p. 14.
[19] Ibid., p. 9.
[20] Ibid., p. 10.

Thus, for example, dimming lights onstage clearly indicates night – this corresponds to the 'Index' category. Aston and Savona also provide a useful glossary: '(i) *icon*: a sign linked by similarity to its object, e.g. a photograph; (ii) *index*: a sign which points to or is connected to its object, e.g. smoke as an index of fire; (iii) *symbol*: a sign where the connection between sign and object is agreed by convention and there is no similarity between object and sign, e.g. the dove as symbol of peace.'[21]

Performance theory and the Death of the Author

The tension between written and performance texts has ironically become additionally vexed by the analytical attention directed at the elements of performance. By sleight-of-thought this leads to a version-in-drama of the Death of the Author: 'Once the "doing" of theatre is reinstated, then the notion of individual authorship is also challenged . . .'[22]

Quite why this has happened is curious. There is no reason, theoretical or otherwise, why such a conclusion should follow. The fact that theatre theorists seem to like the idea that notions of individual authorship have been superseded may stem from a desire to provide a validating equivalent to the popularity of that powerful postmodern conceit, the Death of the Author. Or, perhaps, to insufficient knowledge about the way the writing process works.

Some theorists are aware of an uneasiness: 'One of the major thrusts of reader-response theory is to downplay the centrality of the author in artistic production. Theatre, however, has already long decentralised the playwright on behalf of the producer, director and actors. The generation of meaning in the theatre is more

[21] *Theatre as Sign-System; a Semiotics of Text and Performance* by Elaine Aston and George Savona (Routledge, 1998), p. 6. First published 1991.
[22] Ibid., p. 2.

complex, and involves more kinds of participants, than literary practice does . . .'[23] While this last comment is accurate, it leaves open the matter of how text creation can be addressed, without subsuming it into other functions of drama creation. Ultimately – *pace* chapter 1 – the very expansion of attention in performance theory serves to close down, if not annihilate, the written text and, with it, the significance of the dramatist.

The Death of the Author and the fourth wall

The space between performers and audience is known as the fourth wall, defined in cultural theory by the concept of the 'frame'. This demarcates the space and relations within which the performance takes place, and allows for communication between performance and audience.

In a curious conceptual paradox, devaluing the written script and the dramatist, along with focusing attention on the stage (the frame) from the audience's point of view, has indirectly also displaced attention on to the fourth wall. This is rarely discussed in the theory, perhaps partly to do with a wholesale acceptance of the legacy of Brecht's theory of theatre. His theory – or, perhaps more accurately, politicised intentions for theatre – was, together with his plays, an important influence on the radical drama of the 1960s and 1970s. Antonin Artaud had written passionately about doing away with stage and auditorium, asserting that written dialogue belonged in books, and Brecht himself actively developed forms of writing and performance where members of the cast moved in and out of 'character', to speak directly to the audience (along with other devices, such as captions onstage).

However, rather than doing away with the division between performers and audience, and taking down the fourth wall, such

---

[23] *Theory/Theatre* by Mark Fortier (Routledge, 1997), p. 94.

devices ironically draw attention to it even more. As Herbert Blau has put it, 'Periodically in the theatre we want to reduce this distance, if not abolish it, modulate it for intimacy . . . the fourth wall may be down, or up, but the mural still lingers, and it lingers from the archaic theatre: no matter what it is that we see, in great things or small, something more is being repressed.'[24]

Direct address to the audience focuses attention even more sharply on the fourth wall, that framed and invisible divide between performers and audience. The audience can respond only within strictly demarcated conventions and this shared knowledge is precisely part of the pleasure of testing the fourth wall. At the same time the more it is tested, the more it is reinforced. The fourth wall is never abolished in performance.

Even in a more active interaction between performers and audience, where the latter may come onstage, it is the performers who are always in control. Music-hall heckling and banter are, in some ways, the supreme example of this. The show must always go on. Those who make theatre know this: 'it is sufficient . . . for an actor of power to speak a powerful text for the spectator to be caught up in an illusion, although, of course, he will still know that he is at every instant in a theatre. The aim is not how to avoid illusion . . .'[25]

This is the great excitement of drama: the illusion and the willing collusion in the illusion. The difficulty lies in the acknowledgement that 'there is no constant relation between text and performance in drama'.[26] Herbert Blau has expressed this acknowledgement of illusion in its historical context: 'There is . . . a kind of graduated voyeurism in the history of the theatre. It has to do with how different periods distance themselves from the object being looked at, the body of performance . . .'[27]

---

[24] Ibid., p. 159.
[25] *The Empty Space* by Peter Brook (Penguin, 1977), p. 88.
[26] *Drama in Performance* by Raymond Williams (Penguin, 1972), p. 174.
[27] Blau, op. cit., p. 86.

Audience as active

This does not in any way accede to the idea that the audience (individually or collectively) is 'passive'. The act of reading a book, or watching/hearing a performance, is a supremely active one. If it were not, no one could claim that audiences or readers actually 'create' meaning. Audience members scan, receive the material and process it. Performers onstage detect collective audience responses: the quality of rapt attention, lack of attention in small movements and rustling; more vocally, laughter of many different kinds – all these attest to the activeness of audience response at the moment of performance. The activity continues for the audience after the performance is ended; in discussion, argument, in processing and thinking about the experience.

Conclusions

There is no doubt that the development of performance theory has transformed ways of approaching theatre studies. However, its over-strong demarcation from the praxis of production and performance leads it at times to devalue the written text and the dramatist (even while, ironically, heavily relying on such texts and dramatists to illustrate its work) and, in the interests of a misplaced radicalism, to oversimplify the relations between performance and audience: 'Probably nothing is more fundamental indeed to theatre than the setting off of its particular space from the space of everyday life, so that a potential audience is aware that the material "set off" is to be regarded in a special way.'[28]

For the dramatist, the idea that there can ever be an immutable definition of what it is to write for a particular audience is a

---

[28] 'Indexical Space in the Theatre' by Marvin Carlson (*ASSAPH Studies in the Theatre*, Section C, No. 10; Faculty of Visual and Performing Arts, Tel Aviv University, 1994), p. 2.

distraction from the convention-defined specifics of writing drama.

It is possible to argue that, in a sense, any potential audience is, or will always or inevitably be, inscribed within the text of the play. The cluster of interests, approaches, source material and style of writing, which compose the resources and materials of the dramatist and then become part of the text, 'speak' to the audience. An enhanced consciousness of one's sources is, inevitably, a subliminal sense of 'audience', though it is rarely, if ever, seen in this way. The dramatist has no more direct control over the audience than does a poet or a novelist and can therefore never really either predict the audience's response or second guess it in the writing.

4 The text from the other side: director and performer

Director and performer approach the written text from points of view diametrically opposite to that of the dramatist. First, to state the obvious, they each receive a conceptually completed text, the result of a great deal of time and effort and thought. This does not apply in quite the same way to devised or workshop-written drama. Nevertheless, the dramatist is never a mere scribe or tape recorder. No matter how much material is generated in group processes, there are important moments of separation all the way through when the dramatist's imaginative and conceptual skills take charge. While the dramatist is responsible for every voice and for the overarching shape (structure), the director's responsibility is to the process of mediation between dramatic and performance text, and the performer's responsibility is primarily to his/her own role, in the context of the drama as a whole.

There are parallels between theatre performers and musicians. Each instrumentalist plays his/her own part, with relevant and varying degrees of knowledge of the overall piece. Each plays from written music, with rests where he/she is silent; occasionally there might be a tiny musical cue written in to signal where, in the ensemble piece, his/her contribution comes. The modern theatre performer has the entire script, but learns only his/her part. It is – theoretically – possible for both musician and performer to learn only his/her own part, without regard to the rest of the work.

Whether this produces better or worse performances is a matter for debate.

The director

The director, however, *must* know it all. One of the lesser clichés around is that the director, at his/her best, is there to realise the dramatist's 'vision'. Insofar as this applies to the director's careful reading of, and thinking about, the text, clearly this has some resonance. But it is an unreliable cliché, since it suggests that there is something inherently mystical about the way a director might read through the text, as if the director were a mind reader, trying to second guess the inner thoughts of the dramatist. The director must be able to read, not the dramatist's mind but what is on the page. Of course, there may be matters to clarify/discuss with the dramatist and changes to be made, but unless a director can enter the verbal (i.e., written) drama-on-the-page, the working relationship between dramatist and director is likely to be uncertain, if not difficult.

The director may confer with the dramatist, the two may have very good rapport and the dramatist may be content that the director has read his/her work and understands it well, but in the end the director must take the text and work it within the rehearsal and production process. The author here is clearly not Dead, but merely somewhere else. Unless, that is, she/he is acting in his/her own drama in performance, or even directing it. This tends to be a relatively rare event.

The director carries the most comprehensive aesthetic responsibility – whether as individual director in a production, or as the artistic director of a theatre, responsible for choosing and commissioning new writing. Just as schools of new playwriting develop because of the entrepreneurship and encouragement of directors, so do radical innovations in theories of acting. Edward Braun's history of theatre directors makes this very clear: 'Most of the directors in this book are acknowledged today as major forces in the development of the modern theatre and are identified with the various "traditions" they inaugurated.'[1]

The performer, acting and the text

In the previous chapter, outlining the remits of performance theory, there was one element only referred to in passing: the performer. While most performance-based semiology has addressed the objects on the stage, Elam has offered a more precise, multi-factorial approach, in 'the dialectic between the animate and the inanimate, or, better, between the subjective and the objective on stage. It is almost unavoidable, when thinking about dramatic representation, to draw a firm and automatic distinction between the active subject, embodied by the actor, and the objects to which he relates and which participate in the action through his agency.'[2]

Constantin Stanislavsky, actor and director, evolved what is generally considered to be the basis of modern, realistic stage acting. His book, *An Actor Prepares*, first published in 1936, codified his approach and many of his formulations are now in familiar usage, encapsulating some of the basics of how to approach performance; terms such as units and objectives, emotion memory, the super-objective, are widely used in drama schools and in rehearsals. Stanislavsky's starting point was based on the principle that the physical and emotional were absolutely intertwined. He was convinced that muscular tension interfered with the performer's ability to access and convey 'emotion', and physical and vocal 'warming-up' in rehearsal and before performances is now an assumed practices.

---

[1] Braun, op. cit., p. 201.
[2] Ibid., p. 165.

Perhaps the most widely popularised legacy from Stanislavsky is the idea that the performer must draw from his/her own personal, actual and emotional memories, in order to 'find' emotional and psychological 'truth' to mould into the reality of the character she/he is playing. The concept of 'emotion memory' certainly suggests such a formulation, but the interest and importance of Stanislavsky's work – his theory of performance, as it were – is much more than this.

Work on a play, he suggested, 'begins with the use of *if . . .*' which 'acts as a lever to lift us out of the world of actuality into the realm of imagination'.[3] This is already at a very fundamental remove from the hermetic world of the performer's own experiences. This is followed by a grounding in 'facts': 'Every invention of the actor's imagination must be thoroughly worked out and solidly built on a basis of facts. It must be able to answer all the questions (when, where, why, how) . . .'[4] All this evidence must first be drawn from the written text itself. In drama schools this commonly follows a painstaking process where students first comb the written dramatic text for factual answers to relevant questions. It is only after these have been found (or found not to be present) that more detailed emotional and psychological motivational exploration (i.e., invention) begins to take place.

Stanislavsky's second basic principle lay in a carefully detailed structural analysis of the text, and positioning of the performer/character within that analytical understanding. Segmental analysis of structural elements within scenes, through the concept of units and objectives, takes place within a grasp of the overall shape of the writing: 'The part and the play must not remain in fragments.'[5] Overall, there is a 'super-objective', which he suggested can be formulated relatively simply: 'What is the core of the play

---

[3] *An Actor Prepares*, translated by Elizabeth Reynolds Hapgood (Methuen, 2006), pp. 54 and 46. First published in Britain in 1937.
[4] Ibid., p. 70.
[5] Ibid., p. 115.

– the thing without which it cannot exist? . . . What is essential to it?'[6]

This integrationist approach, of binding together structure and performer is, in different ways, something which both director and performer must carry out: 'In a play the whole stream of individual, minor objectives, all the imaginative thoughts and feelings and actions of an actor, should converge to carry out the *super-objective* of the plot. The common bond must be so strong that even the most insignificant detail, if it is not related to the *super-objective*, will stand out as superfluous or wrong.'[7] Voice and text coach Cicely Berry has confirmed the importance of this structural analysis: 'I think every play has what I call a centre line, and by that I mean the thought which expresses the bottom line of the play, and this centre line is in its way a symbol of the whole.'[8]

The individuated work of the performer, drawing on emotional memory and experience, is then applied to the internality of the performance. With an understanding of the '*through-going action* and the *super-objective* . . .'[9] and a sense of how each moment is part of the whole, the performer must have what is described as a 'point of attention', or a 'circle of attention', which, supremely interestingly, 'must not be in the auditorium' – that is, the focus of the performer's work must be entirely on and within the stage/performance space.[10] The 'objectives', as worked in rehearsal, must, therefore 'be directed toward the other actors, and not towards the spectators'.[11]

We can see here how Brecht's polemical attitude to the drama's effects on an audience seems to be diametrically opposed to the idea of the 'circle of attention'. However, Brecht's own dramas ironically depend precisely on the power of performers to hold their own

[6] Ibid., p. 116.
[7] Ibid., p. 271.
[8] *Text in Action* (Virgin, 2001), p. 254.
[9] Stanislavsky, op. cit., p. 274.
[10] Ibid., p. 75.
[11] Ibid., p. 118.

circle of attention onstage, against which to pitch those elements which seem (by contrast) to be addressed directly to the audience.

The fourth wall

The central paradox of the way performance 'works' takes us back to the concept of the fourth wall: 'If actors really mean to hold the attention of a large audience they must make every effort to maintain an uninterrupted exchange of feelings, thoughts and actions among themselves.'[12] While Stanislavsky is rightly credited with developing 'realistic' performances, which drew on performers' 'personal' experiences and related emotions, at the same time the super-objective of his 'method' (to borrow his own phrase) was to place such results at the service of the imaginative, the fictional, the dramatic 'illusion', as contained within the written text – an impersonal and shared goal – and then contained within the imaginary world onstage.

Returning to the fourth wall from the point of view of the director/performer enables a different focus on this invisible and exciting divider. Herbert Blau's trenchant comment that all experiments in performance, from Brecht onwards, do not abolish the fourth wall, but merely vary the modes of interacting in relation to it, are reinforced from a different perspective. The realm of the imagination, into which the performer leaps as an act of faith (the *if*) is extended into the constructed world of the play, which, paradoxical as it might sometimes seem, is predicated precisely on the shared illusion (the collusion) which is always there between performers and audience. Each side 'pretends' (from their own point of view) that the other is not aware of its presence; at the same time the presence of each is predicated on the presence of the other. Both participate in the '*if*', the one by making it into its performed

[12] Ibid., p. 197.

illusion, the other by watching the prepared work, as if eaves-dropping, as if overlooking.

After Stanislavsky – new objectivism

More recent theatre practitioners, responding to both the benefits and the myths which constitute the legacies of Stanislavsky's approach, have interestingly aimed to reintroduce what one might call an objectivist approach to performance and what happens on the stage. These are different ways of effecting a closer rapprochement with the fundamental fictionality of the onstage world. Declan Donnellan, challenging the supremacy of a totalist interiorising psychological and emotional approach, has asserted that the performer should always direct everything to a 'target': 'The target is always specific . . . The target is always transforming . . . The target is always active . . .'[13] Like Stanislavsky, however, he reinforces the 'attention' needed from the performer and directed to another performer onstage: 'The target always exists outside, and at a measurable distance . . .'[14]

David Mamet, actor, playwright and director, has been even more down to earth and matter of fact, declaring that the 'Stanislavsky "Method" and the technique of the schools derived from it, is nonsense'.[15] Provocatively, and usefully, he has asserted, 'The actor is onstage to communicate the play to the audience. That is the beginning and the end of his and her job. To do so the actor needs a strong voice, superb diction, a supple, well-proportioned body, and rudimentary understanding of the play.'[16]

Mamet's reaction to the mystique created by the idea that the character, the personality and personal experience of the performer

[13] *The Actor and the Target* (Nick Hern Books, 2005), pp. 22, 23, 24.
[14] Ibid., p. 20.
[15] *True and False* (Vintage, 1999), p. 6. First published 1997.
[16] Ibid., p. 9.

are somehow welded together is directly informed by his experiences as dramatist and director: 'When the actual courage of the actor is coupled with the lines of the playwright, the illusion of character is created. . . . There is no character. There are just lines on the page.'[17] While not referring directly to the concept of the circle of attention onstage, Mamet has implied it in his assertion that the actor should be 'outwardly directed . . . The more a person's concentration is outward, the prematurely interesting that person becomes.'[18]

All these reinforce the imperative of the self-contained relative autonomy of performance, transmuted across the fourth wall. Both in the shared timescale of the performance space and time continuum, there is (whatever the internal chronology of the narrative) the immediacy of the moment of performance (live or recorded). The stress is on the immediacy of the here and now, the fleeting, constantly fleeting presentness of performance. As Keith Johnstone remarked in his book, *Impro for Storytellers*, 'I tried to keep the students' attention on what was actually happening, rather than on what had already happened or was about to.'[19]

Conclusions: performance and immediacy

Directors and performers are, at all times, aware of the immediacy, of the present-ness of the moment of performance, of an illusion of spontaneity, which must be carefully prepared in rehearsal and re-created in every performance, or for every take in recorded drama. As we shall see later, this consists of a distinctive approach to the representation of time, which is carried by the voice and body of the performer. It is via this medium that meanings are conveyed, however (and by whomever) they are then interpreted: as Raymond

[17] Ibid., pp. 52 and 21.
[18] Ibid., p. 95.
[19] Faber, 1999, p. 155. First published 1994.

Williams pointed out: 'Every aspect of the performance is governed by the denotation-connotation dialectic etc.: the set, the actor's body, his movements and speech determine and are determined by a constantly shifting network of primary and secondary meanings,'[20] and Keir Elam developed this to remind us that in the Western performance tradition, the 'apex of the hierarchy is occupied by the actor'.[21]

---

[20] *Writing in Society* (Verso, 1991), p. 11.
[21] Elam, op. cit., p. 17.

5 The novel and the drama

As part of the preparation for, and exploration of, writing drama, a writerly awareness of the distinction between the novel and the drama as literary conventions is crucial. Some of this understanding can (and should) be gained from literature study and analysis. However, this understanding needs to be experienced and 'learned' anew within the practice of writing itself. The student needs to know the distinction between the novel and the drama in moving from his/her imagination to the page, from the perspective of the praxis of writing – a combination of theory and practice. In turn, this understanding needs to be translated and infused into work in the classroom/seminar. Some of the distinctions direct us back to the so-called 'problem' of how to read (and, by extrapolation, how to write) the dramatic text.

This is compounded by the question of how the dramatist 'thinks' the relationship between the written text and the performance 'text'. In our culture the novel is still the dominant literary form, defining reading habits (and purchases and popularity) and conventions of narrative and storytelling. Critical approaches to drama are heavily influenced by literary-critical approaches to the novel and often the same issues arise in both, though reflected in a differentiated terminology.

Size matters

To begin with (to state the obvious), the drama contains fewer words than the novel. The average-length novel is likely to be around 80,000 words; the drama (for evening stage performance) around 20,000 words and, in the case of film, where dialogue forms a small amount of the final scripted text, there are even fewer words devoted to what appears as speech. So, while the scope, the imaginative world, the subject matter and themes etc. addressed by the dramatist may be as major/significant as those addressed by the novelist, there are fewer words in which to contain and convey the material.

This relative concision implies the application of a distilling imagination, which is sometimes similar to the way in which the poet, rather than the novelist, might work. However, both dramatist and novelist have to think about matters of narrative and ordering. This does not, I must stress, mean that each does or should just write 'realism' or 'naturalism', only that, at base, both the drama and the novel are predominantly narrative-based fictional genres, in a way that poetry is not.

In terms of distribution and consumption, the distinctions between novel and drama are major. Novels are bought as individual artefacts and read idiosyncratically; a bit at a time, different amounts at each reading, with the reader in complete control of this process. Pages can be reread, the reader can refer back, or leap ahead. The reader can start anywhere – 'cheat' and go to the end, before returning to see how the novel gets there. By contrast, in performance a play is seen and heard at one sitting, in a designated location, alongside other people: the individual reader has become a member of an audience.

The audience must see the event in the order in which it is produced and presented. Even with the advantages of video and DVD, where novel-like control is a possibility, the same principle largely operates. After the event, each member of the audience relies on memory for further thought and discussion. Even if the dramatic text is published and can be read, it cannot reproduce the experienced performance. It can act as an aide-memoire to the performance, of course, but it also produces a new reading experience in its own right.

There is a one-to-one 'intimacy' created between reader and novel (or between reader and dramatic text) which is very different from the collective experience of being a member of an audience. This can be exciting and also a mixed blessing. Extraneous sounds in a theatre or cinema (coughing, paper-rustling) can disturb the concentration of other audience members in our Western convention, where certain codes of behaviour are expected. In other cultures and other situations performances often take place with audience noise (families eating, people wandering in and out, sometimes heckling). I remember an account of a production of *Hamlet* given in a small village in the Middle East, performed on an improvised scaffold, with everyone sitting on the ground with a local cast. At Hamlet's death, the audience cheered and applauded, and would not allow the play to proceed until the scene had been replayed and the actor had 'died' all over again.

The immediacy of the theatrical experience (the play happening at the level of different kinds of 'presentness' time frames), gives a clue to some of the features which attract people to write drama, as against, or sometimes alongside, writing prose fiction and poetry. Playwright Howard Barker wrote that he 'came to theatre . . . because I would write speech and was impatient with novels . . .'[1] Playwright Sheila Yeger linked an enthusiasm for writing drama to the excitement of performance: 'I can't imagine why anyone would decide to write a play, as opposed to a story, a poem or a novel, unless they had already experienced as spectator, or possibly actor, the extraordinary power of theatre, unless they had been part of an audience and become involved in that unique transaction, where the

[1] *Arguments for a Theatre* (Manchester, 1993), p. 24.

actors agree to pretend to be these people, say these things, do these things, if the audience will agree to believe in them totally.'[2]

Narrative voice, point of view, character and subjectivity

The dramatist has a very different task from the novelist in the way she/he deploys language in the imaginative text. David Lodge, novelist, dramatist and academic, with experience of writing in different forms and genres, has pointed to one critical difference in the dramatist's working process, which is that the novelist retains 'absolute' control over the text, until it is published.[3] Referring also to the centrality of singular-voiced narration (even where there is more than one narrative point of view), Lodge argued that, as a result, 'The dramatic form is much more impartial, and there is no authorial voice in the drama text which may betray a sympathy for one character over another.'[4] Because of this, he suggested, 'The novel . . . is . . . the best equipped to represent thought, and therefore the subjectivity of experience.'[5]

This is a complex idea, with resonances which are debatable in terms of what they suggest about 'character' and narrative point of view. Narrative in the novel can, of course, suggest thoughts, emotions, what is commonly referred to as the 'inner life' of characters, whether it is in the first or the third person, in a far more direct way than their equivalents in drama. However, this does not necessarily lead to the conclusion that the novel is any more 'subjective' or 'objective' than the drama. The single-narrative voice may suggest a conflation between authorial voice and the 'real-life' experiences or thoughts or feelings of the real-life author, but this is

[2] *The Sound of One Hand Clapping* (Amber Lane Press, 1990), p. 16.
[3] *The Practice of Writing* (Secker & Warburg, 1996), p. 205.
[4] Ibid., p. 209.
[5] Ibid., p. 208.

the special illusion which belongs to prose fiction. It is, in any case, never a provable (nor, often, a very interesting) correlation.

In the end, it comes down to the question of how the language is deployed and how human agency (i.e., character) is represented and realised in the two distinctive conventions. The distinction, as far as narrative point of view is concerned, is critical: 'In the theatre we have no controlling narrative voice. What we do have is a variety of points of view . . . the shifting point of view is a central and eternal truth of theatre . . . a built-in reality.'[6] It could, in fact, be argued that the mono-vocal (ego-centred) basis of dialogue in drama, as against the poly-vocal (narrative plus character) voicing in prose fiction, provides an even more transparent access to apparent 'subjectivity'. However, this depends on the definitions of subjectivity which operate, and how they are assumed to be refracted in imaginative writing via the representation of 'individual' human beings; as we shall see (chapters 7 and 13), in the analysis of the literary fabric of the drama, subjectivity as such cannot ever be the primary focus in drama.

'Subjectivity', insofar as it is represented through the agency of character and/or performer in the drama, is differently written, differently inscribed in the text through the form and devices of the writing itself. Thus anything 'imagined' (i.e., in the mind, in the imagination) could potentially be written as poem, story, novel or drama. To elect and proceed with the dramatic mode of writing is to transform imagination onto the page, deploying a particular kind of mental/imaginative skill, which is then translated into a particular literary convention – however much or little it may also be informed by an understanding of performance. This has a spin-off effect on the different ways in which readers/audiences 'read' the relevant artefact: 'In most novels, the reader is, so to speak, personally conducted, the author is our guide. In the drama, so far as the dramatist is concerned, we must travel alone.'[7]

[6] *The Playwright's Guidebook* by Stuart Spencer (Faber, 2002), p. 12.
[7] Baker, op. cit., p. 7.

Poly-vocality and the dialogic

The work of Bakhtin has come back into prominence in the past two decades because of the way in which his socio-linguistic insights have influenced analytical approaches to the novel. In general, literary theory has paid less attention to drama than it has to the novel and, from the point of view of Bakhtinian terminology, there are certain categories which allow of some extrapolation towards drama, even though he did not explicitly write about the genre. According to Michael Holquist, 'Bakhtin's search . . . led him to explore parallels between the conditions at work when any of us speaks in the most common everyday situation on the one hand, and on the other, conditions that obtain when an author writes what we call a literary work.'[8]

Bakhtin is responsible for a term which is now widely used and which, for obvious reasons, suggests a link with drama: this is 'dialogism'. According to Holquist, the term 'dialogism' was never actually used by Bakhtin himself, but 'Dialogue is an obvious master key to the assumptions that guided Bakhtin's work', from his thinking as philosopher and linguist. In particular, he conceptualised the relationship between individual consciousness (and its different forms of expression in the world) and the society (historical and contemporary) within which it functioned. In terms of literary artefacts, there is a complex dialogic relationship between the world and the individual creating consciousness, and there is also a complex dialogic process, which takes place within the work itself. This comes down to the function and uses of language. For Bakhtin, 'the dialogic concept of language he proposes is fundamental.'[9]

---

[8] *Dialogism: Bakhtin and his World* by Michael Holquist (Routledge, 1990), p. 13.
[9] Ibid., p. 15.

Narrative, structure and causality

There is an interesting structural imperative, which follows from the (relatively) shorter length of the drama (fewer words). The optimum length of prose fiction is really the same question as 'how long is a piece of string'. It can be a short story (how long is a short story?), it can be what we characterise as a novella – somewhere between a short story and a 'full-length' novel, which itself can be, etc., etc. Because of this architectonic flexibility, narrative in the novel can expand at will to include detail of a kind not necessary or relevant to drama. This degree of flexibility, as well as the power of the narrative voice, points to different ways of constructing causality in prose fiction and drama.

Longer prose fiction is structured in 'chapters'; their equivalents in drama are scenes, traditionally (but not always) organised into larger groups of acts. This structuring has both extrinsic and intrinsic implications. From within the drama itself, each scene is characterised generally by a change in time and/or place. This corresponds to the practical imperative of having to change or modify the stage set. Chapter distinctions may correspond with these, or they may simply be 'rests' between different moments of the same event or series of events. Writing nearly a century before Hayman, Baker commented that as far as drama is concerned, 'This needed swiftness requires methods of making effects more obviously and more emphatically than in the novel.'[10] Such distinct appropriations of genre in relation to the imagination and literary uses of language are of profound importance for the dramatist who, in the end, imagines and writes exclusively in dialogue.

[10] Baker, op. cit., p. 6.

6 Methods of teaching – the workshop

Teaching the art of writing drama mostly takes place in higher education, like other creative writing teaching, in classes generally called workshops. This term evokes the idea of the craft-based workshop, where functional objects (chairs, tables) as well as artefacts (decorative pottery) might be made. Fine art teaching has its own term for the places where paintings or sculpture are made – the studio. Above all, these terms draw attention to the fact that something new is being made, created, which has connections with both art and craft.

The term 'workshop', however, has more than a history associated with other arts and crafts. In the context of creative writing it is packed with various ideological and methodological assumptions about what sort of activity goes on and what its purpose is. In creative writing classes the main activity of the workshop consists of students bringing in fragments of incomplete writing to be subjected to the critical responses of the class and the tutor.

Thus, the creative writing workshop exists in two senses: the Workshop, referring to the institutional distinctiveness of Creative Writing (CW) as an academic discipline, and the verb, to workshop, referring to the practices and methodologies of CW pedagogy. Student writing is 'workshopped'. The pedagogy of drama in higher education owes a great deal to the ideologies which inform general creative writing teaching, along with the practical ways in which post-1960s theatre combined elements of otherwise discrete skills in conceiving, preparing and rehearsing drama for performance.[1]

Early workshop history

The dominant model for the CW workshop was developed at the University of Iowa. The university's first taught course in 'Verse Making' in the spring of 1897 set a precedent, which helped to pave the way for 'creative' work to be submitted as part of the requirements of postgraduate Masters (*sic*) degrees in the 1920s.[2] Stephen Wilbers, historian of the Iowa Writers' Workshop, suggested that some of the protocols of the CW workshop originated in local writers' clubs: 'Their purpose was to improve the participants' skills as writers by allowing each member to have a turn reading his or her original work, after which the group would respond with suggestions and literary criticism . . . Accordingly, the method (later to be called the "workshop" approach) was adopted by the University when it offered its first course in creative writing . . .'[3]

Norman Foerster, director of the Iowa School of Letters (1930–44), succeeded in getting the creative dissertation accepted for the Ph.D. degree in the early 1930s and in 1939 the title 'Writers' Workshops' was officially used for the first time. In 1949 the Iowa English Department incorporated CW into its undergraduate English Major. The consolidation of Iowa's achievements in the 1940s and 1950s, under director Paul Engle (1942–66), led to the Iowa Writers' Workshop becoming, in effect, the prototype for CW courses in the US during the 1960s, often founded and run by Iowa Workshop graduates.

[1] For a detailed history of Creative Writing in the UK, see *The Author is not Dead, Merely Somewhere Else* by Michelene Wandor (Palgrave Macmillan, 2008).
[2] *The Iowa Writers' Workshop* by Stephen Wilbers (University of Iowa Press, 1980); *Seven Decades of the Iowa Workshop*, ed. Tom Grimes (Hyperion, New York, 1999).
[3] Wilbers, op. cit., p. 19.

The tutorial precedent

In academic terms the workshop is also another word for the seminar: small-group teaching, which aims to maximise student participation. Interestingly, the university seminar originates from both ends of the educational class spectrum. In the nineteenth century, principles of self-government were reflected in classes in the Co-operative and adult education movements. The 'tutorial class', which became the pedagogic method for this movement, was developed by the University Extension movement and took its teaching model from the oldest-established universities of Oxford and Cambridge, making a distinction between mass lectures and the small group.

CW was more easily established in the US, in part because when English became a degree subject in its own right, supplanting the study of Classics and Philology, it retained some of the elements from both in the subjects of Composition and Rhetoric. These became, and still are, compulsory forms of writing instruction for all first-year university students. We have no equivalent to this in UK higher education. Composition acted as a disciplinary bridge in the US when CW was first taught in the 1920s.

CW took longer to arrive in the UK (the best part of a century, in any formal sense). However, community writing and informal professional writers' groups were not unknown. In 'The Teaching of Creative Writing', Philip Hobsbaum reminisced back to the early 1950s. As a Cambridge undergraduate at Downing College, Cambridge, where F. R. Leavis taught, Hobsbaum organised a writing group in 1952, typing out copies of poems and stories, and sending them round beforehand for members to read. In 1955 he started a similar group in London, and subsequently 'managed' (as he put it) others in Belfast and Glasgow. He described part of his role: 'I usually let the discussion polarise to some extent before intervening . . . it was a matter of avoiding closure.'[4]

[4] *Teaching Creative Writing* eds. Moira Monteith and Robert Miles (Open University Press, 1992), p. 30.

Workshop pedagogy

The seminar, or small-group pedagogy in higher education, became particularly important during the 1970s, drawing on ideas derived from principles of political democratisation, community-based creativity and radical work in psychotherapy. A university-based organisation called DUET (Developing University English Teaching) was founded in 1979 by Professor John Broadbent: 'In the later 1960s at Cambridge I was tiring of one-to-one tutorials, so I began holding seminars. Then I moved to the University of East Anglia where the basic teaching unit was the seminar . . . people came late to classes or not at all, hadn't read the books, did not participate or talked demotically. . . . In an effort to get out of this, I regressed to techniques used in primary schools – thematic topics, dramatic improvisation . . .'[5] Broadbent and his colleagues set up conferences and workshops, to explore group dynamics and to increase the degree of student participation, as well as to involve teachers themselves more closely in the classroom process.

Authority

Authority, leadership, democratic participation and a degree of autodidacticism were the socio-political issues at the heart of these various small group activities, infused with many of the ideals in the widespread political and cultural radicalism of the 1960s and 1970s. Feminism, in particular, but not exclusively, placed great importance on the idea of leaderlessness, on equal participation by every member of the group, on the democracy of experience and voice. The equation of leaderlessness with democracy, based on the desire to overthrow what were seen as oppressive traditions of power, was shared by many theatre groups.

[5] ' "Forms of life": how the DUET project began' by John Broadbent, in *Developing University English Teaching*, ed. Colin Evans (The Edwin Mellen Press, 1995), p. 18.

It was exhilarating, empowering and produced original work, but there were also often competing differences, which were frequently ignored or covered over. Each individual inevitably brought his/her own history and agenda (class, culture, ethnicity, expectations, needs) into the process. While this was precisely the source of much new discovery and creativity, it also became the source of a different kind of organisational difficulty. Power relations, and the important matters of different skills and aims, could not be easily put aside.

The problems inherent in the supposed 'structurelessness' of such groups was analysed in an American feminist magazine, *the second wave*, in 1972:

Any group of people of whatever nature that comes together for any length of time for any purpose will inevitably structure itself in some fashion . . . to strive for a structureless group is as useful, and as deceptive, as to aim at an 'objective' news story, 'value-free' social science or a 'free' economy . . . the idea of 'structurelessness' does not prevent the formation of informal structures, only formal ones . . . As long as the structure of the group is informal, the rules of how decisions are made are known only to a few and awareness of power is limited to those who know the rules . . . The rules of decision-making must be open and available to everyone, and this can happen only if they are formalised.'[6]

The continuing influence of a crude egalitarian ideology has a significant place in the various pedagogic models which have informed the development of CW pedagogy, and it is these which currently influence the way drama is incorporated into higher education.

[6] By Joreen, vol. 2, no. 1, 1972, pp. 20–1.

Workshop practice and power relations

As was briefly mentioned in the Introduction, the first full post-graduate CW course in the UK was the MA set up at the University of East Anglia, for novel writing. Various teachers and writers in other universities were already including aspects of CW in their literature teaching, but it took far longer for CW to spread more widely. It was not until the end of the 1980s, when the two-tier higher education system was homogenised, that disciplinary and ideological spaces were available for a new, practical subject such as CW. Before the end of this decade, higher education was divided between universities, polytechnics and colleges of further education (the latter also took in younger students). Polytechnics became known as universities and because their remit was more flexible (often practical and vocational) than universities, the idea of CW as a subject found a more easily assimilated place in the curriculum.

Pivotal to CW workshop protocol, and seen as constituting its distinctive professional practice, is a special form of 'criticism', or critiquing. This applies to both under- and postgraduate workshops. As Danny Broderick has described, in the 'seminar/workshop . . . students' own work in progress is reviewed and revised through critical discussion . . . This cooperative critiquing of work by peers . . . places emphasis on the analysis of the text as literary artefact . . . Students are asked to make value judgements on their own and each others' texts as part of the process of arriving at the artefact.'[7]

In the process of 'workshopping', therefore, the CW seminar is driven by procedures of *rewriting*, rather than writing. In addition, the process of critiquing, and the stress on rewriting, draws on literary-critical criteria, which were developed over decades to interpret and evaluate complete and published pieces of work in poetry and the novel. This lends the flattering illusion that the workshop somehow duplicates the professional publishing (or

[7] Danny Broderick, NAWE website, 1999.

theatre-producing) process, or that it is a latter-day version of the master (*sic*)–apprentice relationship. The conditions of teaching and learning, whatever they may or may not lead to, are quite different from any professional artistic situation, and – among other things – serve to conceal the fact that the real pedagogic object of such a class/workshop is the process of learning to produce a certain kind of imaginative writing, rather than directly training professional writers.

Criticism and value judgement

If the main pedagogic activity in the workshop is 'criticism', there must be some kind of informing criteria and value judgements at stake. In the workshop, such value judgements are inevitably concealed, because rarely, if at all, explicitly taught or shared. At the very least, there is simply not the time. Where CW is taught as part of the content of English undergraduate degrees there are likely to be some shared contexts, but this is by no means always the case, even on postgraduate degrees.

Students are often admitted to such courses on the basis of a sample of their writing. This is a half-open-door policy, to enable anyone who is interested in imaginative writing to study and is a good principle for widespread access. However, it can all too easily result in pedagogic problems within the course, because no shared background knowledge or experience can be assumed. In such a context it is far easier for the 'teaching' to be pragmatic and ad hoc, based largely on whatever happens to be brought into the class by the students. Teachers use their expertise to busk. While this seems to construct a student-centred pedagogy, it also creates a contra-dictory state of affairs because, at the same time, the tutor is always in charge and always makes the final assessment. The earlier comments about the disingenuousness about the idea of a 'structureless' class are clearly illustrated.

Given that the bulk of workshop time is given over to discussing student writing, it is virtually impossible, in any thorough-going way, to establish generally understood and shared criteria. The CW literature largely consists of how-to advice, based on generating writing, rather than, on the whole, theorising its critical values. The workshop methodology is built round 'feedback' or 'critiquing', claiming to focus on 'process' rather than 'product'.

There is a particular vocabulary, which has evolved in relation to CW pedagogy. 'Feedback' can mean favourable or adverse opinion (this is 'good' or 'bad'). 'Criticism' or 'critiquing' can be (often is) used in the colloquial sense of put-down, disapproval. The solution of offering 'constructive' or 'positive' criticism means saying nice things first, pointing out what you 'like', what you think is 'good'. This is contrasted with its opposite, 'negative' criticism, which involves pointing out what is 'wrong' or what doesn't 'work'. The mooted ideal is to find some form of 'constructive criticism', which is meant to 'help' the student rewrite his/her work, if he/she wants to. It is a kind of on-the-spot reader response which, while it may well elicit the odd useful comment, cannot possibly be elevated into a serious methodology (let alone any poetics of writing) for understanding and teaching what is involved in imaginative writing.

Training professional writers versus self-expression

An ideological confusion underpins workshop practice. Part of the legacy of CW pedagogy derives from its US origins in the postgraduate workshop. Initially, as an advanced academic course, CW had ambitions to train students to become professional writers. This aim was echoed in the first MA in the UK, where writer/academics Malcolm Bradbury and Angus Wilson consciously wished to provide an opportunity for would-be professional writers to have a space in which to develop their art and craft as novelists.

While this might be a perfectly laudable aim in a very specialised context, the problem is that it has continued to be the informing principle, the shop window, as it were, of most CW courses in an expanding field. The claim (though not the promise) that CW can train professional writers has remained the headline attraction for students, as well as the genuine (if misplaced) ambition of many teachers. This principle retains the idea expressed in many CW books (including how-to drama-writing texts) that such training only produces results if the student has 'talent'.

By comparison with other, longer-established, academic 'Humanities' subjects, this is clearly a risky idea. Such academic courses, while always subject- or discipline-specific, do not, on the whole, directly train for successful (vocational) employment. They focus on the parameters of the subject and on a consensus agreed over time (notwithstanding the fact that this also changes) about what a curriculum consists of and how it is assessed. The long-standing educational debate about 'vocational' versus 'academic' courses is not merely an argument about manual versus intellectual training, but also a discussion about how directly 'applied' such training is and can be, in terms of the job market.

The other side of the CW coin, also much bruited in how-to books, is that all imaginative writing is a form of self-expression. The idea that imaginative writing literally 'expresses' the 'self' is behind some of the comments quoted in the next chapter – about the dramatist's subject matter coming from his/her own experience and the idea that the blank page is a terrifying obstacle to be overcome. This attitude, including the overwhelming stress on personal experience, good or traumatic, memory, dreams and the real people in the student's life, as the source of imaginative raw material, serves to transform the workshop into an arena where personal, emotional and sometimes traumatic material may be 'revealed' and discussed. Inevitably, such an emotionally risky enterprise suggests that the workshop has much in common with a therapy group where writing is one of the methods behind a kind of 'healing'.

This has rather different, problematic and, I suggest, irre-concilable problems, when combined with the Romantic/training professional/great writers claim. If CW is training professional writers (those who already have 'talent'), then the great-writers approach privileges the text over the writer; if students are taught that CW expresses the self (writing as therapy), then the person is privileged over the writing. The first overvalues the art, the second overvalues the person, and together they confuse the object of the work and its objectives. They cannot be simultaneously and effectively contained within the same pedagogic model. Both, of course, evade the fundamental issues of what is involved in the actual process of imaginative (dramatic) writing.

The workshop as a House of Correction

The methodology of the workshop is widely accepted. However, even in accounts of it by those who work according to its principles there are very clear problems. For example, Tom Grimes, in *Seven Decades of the Iowa Workshop*, described the internal dynamics of the workshop experience as follows: 'Nearly every participant has sensed and reacted with some apprehension to a spirit of com-petition in the Workshop setting. But many writers view the ordeal of measuring their talent against the talent of others as a necessary crisis in their artistic development. Paul Engle believes that the intensity of this experience contributes to the writer's growth.'[8]

The idea that the best way to learn an art form is via an ordeal involving a 'necessary crisis' is, to say the least, punitive. The patronising of individual vulnerability alongside a method which cannot fail but be discouraging and educationally disempowering is not a context in which genuine teaching and learning can take place. Such workshops are sado-masochistic Houses of Correction on a

[8] Grimes, op. cit., p. 131.

Victorian scale. The workshop principles alternate hard-cop/soft-cop methodologies. Training great writers entails toughening them up to 'take criticism', to survive baptisms of fire. In writing-as-therapy (deriving from the idea that writing is self-expression) the emphasis is on avoiding hurting people's feelings (after all, if the writing is thought to be expressing the 'self', then the 'self' will be vulnerable).

Over the past two decades there has been some questioning of the workshop methodology – mostly from America and from teachers who have experience in teaching both Composition (discursive writing) as well as CW. In this country a research project into community writing groups, undertaken in 1992, yielded some interesting insights. Rebecca O'Rourke, author of the study, concluded that 'People are working with cobbled together models of constructive criticism drawn from school – criticism as negative, unpleasant and fault finding – and from the market – criticism as a selective judgement. I found few models drawn from the writing process – criticism as a means to extend, clarify and challenge the writer . . .'[9]

She reported concerns about 'feedback' and 'criticism': 'A contradiction began to emerge. People went to writing groups in order to get feedback on their work and yet were almost always unhappy with the feedback they received. The issue was partly a question of whose responsibility criticism was seen to be: did it belong to the writer, the group or its leader/tutor . . . Some . . . felt encouragement was incompatible with criticising work.'[10] These comments were not voiced within the workshops, but away from it, to her, as someone safely outside the group: 'The language which people used to describe feedback was distinctive and it was at odds with the actual process I observed. The language was violent and aggressive. Phrases such as "rip it to pieces", "pull it part", "pull no punches", "give it the once over" and "brutally honest" . . . It

[9] 'Writing in Education' (NAWE, Autumn 1994).
[10] Ibid.

conjured up a process in which the writing and the writer's feelings were literally taken apart.'[11]

Students wanted more guidelines from the tutors: 'Tension surrounding feedback and criticism was a constant theme in the life of the creative writing groups and courses. It was cited as the most important aspect of the activity, and the one people wanted most to change.'[12] Students were aware that peer comments came (inevitably) from inadequately informed responses – 'many students do not trust the judgement of their peers. . . .'[13] Students, quite rightly, wanted tutors to teach, to take responsibility – 'to deal in absolutes – what was right and what was wrong, good or bad – and to offer definite opinions'.[14]

O'Rourke's conclusion was that 'Central to the problem are issues of power and authority within courses/groups . . .' This is very clear indeed, both from the conflictual pedagogic models into which CW is constrained to fit and from the frankly brutal process to which students can be subjected. It suggests a dynamic which has more than a little in common with a sado-masochistic teacher–student relationship. The student wants approval from the teacher/expert, and at the same time believes that the only valid teacherly comment is disapproval: 'Be brutally honest with me; I can take it.' Because, of course, being able to 'take it' is seen as entering the privileged world of the professional writer. Brutal honesty thus becomes desirable as the most important part of a pedagogic process, which is meant to produce results.

The workshop as therapy group

From another point of view, related to the idea that CW is a form of

[11] *Creative Writing; education, culture and community* (NIACE, 2005), p. 211.
[12] Ibid., p. 206.
[13] Ibid., p. 133.
[14] Ibid., p. 156.

self-expression, Celia Hunt and Fiona Sampson have suggested: 'Creative Writing classes may become, on occasion, arenas where deep feelings and emotions are unearthed and expressed, and teachers and group leaders may sometimes find themselves in the position of counsellor or therapist, without the appropriate skills to act as such.'[15] Teachers need 'to be aware of the importance of creating in the classroom a "holding environment", to use Winnicott's term, within which participants can feel safe enough to engage more closely with their inner worlds. This can be done by organising peer support within the writing group itself, or through the availability of individual consultations with the tutor, or by having available counselling or psychotherapeutic backup which can be used when necessary.'[16] This conflates pedagogic and therapeutic structures and procedures, and gives CW teachers an impossible – if not emotionally dangerous – responsibility.

These conflictual pedagogic models are shoehorned into a practice that renders the workshop a house of correction, built round *rewriting*, rather than writing. Untheorised (or, at best, very under-theorised) principles of 'criticism' are translated into by turns brutal and patronising exchanges. This devolves the conceptual oppositions into the student–teacher relationship, as well as in CW's relationship to its own histories – those of literature, literary criticism and literary theory. The apparent sanctuary within which creativity is supposed to flourish turns out to be a repository for a set of emperor's clothes, which do not fit. It is in this academic context that teaching and learning the art of writing drama takes place.

Theatre workshops

Joan Littlewood's pioneering work at the Theatre Royal, Stratford

[15] *The Self on the Page*, ed. Celia Hunt and Fiona Sampson (Jessica Kingsley, 1998, 2002), p. 12.
[16] Ibid., p. 33.

East in London was called 'Theatre Workshop', and 'workshop plays' became a characteristic label for a great variety of theatre work during the 1960s and 1970s. However, the egalitarian process of the political/alternative theatre movement of the 1960s and 1970s had an ironically paradoxical relationship to writers. On the one hand there was much talk of removing the so-called tyranny of the dramatist (and the director). On the other hand, after a period when all skills, including writing, were taken on by everyone in the group, groups began to acknowledge that writing was a skill that was important in its own right. Writers were then brought into, and participated in, the group devising process. This was productive in a different way, and raised some interesting, and not always comfortable, questions about who 'owned' the text. The individual writer might have put the words on paper, but the members of the group (who were, in fact, employing the writer) also often wanted control of the content and the performance's 'message'.

Although much was made of sharing all skills, in practice these groups tended to be performer dominated – inevitably, because of the numbers involved. This gave performers valuable experience of control in deciding on the subjects of plays and on the 'message' they contained, a contrast to their relative powerlessness in the rest of the professional theatre. It also meant deciding where touring shows were performed and building active relationships with audiences before, during the shows, and/or in discussions at the end of the performance. Theatre in Education groups created plays about specific subjects, targeted at particular age groups; performed in schools, they often had, and still have, an active relationship to many of the subjects or topics taught more formally in the classroom.

As has already been mentioned earlier, some of this work was influenced by visits from companies from other countries. For example, a visit by the American La Mama company in 1967 influenced director Max Stafford-Clark, who ran the Traverse Theatre Workshop in Edinburgh from 1969 to 1972. He brought writers (sometimes teams of writers) together with the performers. He was not the only one to work in one of a range of versions of this participatory group approach: 'The process of shaping or creating a script during rehearsals, of relying on the ideas of a whole company rather than upon an individual writer, has played a decisive part in the activities of the fringe since 1968.'[17] Subsequently, Stafford-Clark set up the Joint Stock theatre company in the early 1970s, where he continued to work in this way. A writer and subject matter were decided on, then a company of performers hired and everyone (with Stafford-Clark as overall director) researched, discussed and improvised for a number of weeks. After this the writer went away and wrote the play, drawing on the previous group work as she/he wished. The same company then rehearsed and performed the play. At the end of the process the play was credited to the individual dramatist, rather that to the whole company.

This way of working was slightly different from the more overtly campaigning, radical political theatre groups, such as Red Ladder, or the Women's Theatre Group. Where Joint Stock always retained the traditional roles of director and writer, these other groups worked for some time on the principle that everyone could do anything, with each person developing all the skills needed to prepare and perform a theatre piece. Red Ladder emerged from a London group called Agitprop, which initially produced posters, leaflets and pamphlets. The group took the name because they used a red ladder in one of their early shows, to illustrate the hierarchy of class.

Conclusions

Of course, all these approaches are entirely valid; they are often exciting, stimulating and skill-expanding. However, they have never supplanted the traditional writerly role for more than a short period

[17] *Disrupting the Spectacle* by Peter Ansorge (Pitman, 1975), pp. 47–8.

of time. In the right circumstances such group-devising practices can be useful for writers to learn 'from within', as it were, about production and performance, but they teach little or nothing about the art of writing drama as a skill in its own imaginative and literary right. For new and/or young writers, such work can be immensely valuable, and it is telling that for virtually all the professional dramatists who began their work in this way there came a point where their own imaginations and decisions about writing became paramount.

This is not because they learned all the necessary skills and could then branch out on their own, nor that they acceded to the dreadful bourgeois individualism of narcissistic literary production. It was (is), rather, that often, precisely because of the experience of trying to merge imaginations and forms of expression in writing and performance (different systems of signification, as the semiologists would say), important realisations were made. These consist of an understanding that while we all live, experience, think, imagine and write in cultural contexts, the location for the melting pot which processes and individuates the shared context is the dramatist's imagination. Writing is fundamentally a solitary job, whatever the form.

Different ways of working are not intrinsically opposed. Students of writing drama benefit a great deal from working with, interacting and acquiring some training in performance and directing, but this is only likely to be possible in drama colleges, where practical performance-based work is part of what's on offer, or in a 'workshop' context offered by a theatre/company. But even within this kind of context, each imagination and intellect must come to terms with its own resources and the skills entailed in writing cannot be collapsed into, or confused with, the skills entailed in per-formance and production. The conceptual and imaginative work necessary for written work of any complexity may coexist with, but can never be superseded by, group work. The art of writing drama is, in the end, not a collaborative art.

7 The concepts in how-to books on dramatic writing

The *poeisis* of drama (the making/writing of the dramatic text) has its own how-to literature. Books about writing film scripts tend to be format and formula driven, generally on market-based models of successful Hollywood films. It goes (almost) without saying, that even following these models meticulously will not necessarily result in a script which will be bought and filmed.

Analysing the foundation blocks of drama-writing books is an interesting exercise. Each book, implicitly or explicitly, lays down a set of principles, on the basis of which the author recommends certain approaches to the act and art of writing. Since the drive behind the books (as with all creative writing texts) is practical – to guide people into writing drama – theorisation of the practice of dramatic writing rarely figures consistently. Distilling and analysing the principles conveyed by the books is important, and also provides some succinct material for discussion in class.

Some basic rubrics cross-reference (consciously or not) approaches to writing prose fiction. Both genres share certain identifying structural features and issues concerning content or subject matter. At the most basic level, the matter of narrative, or story, or plot (whatever the niceties of distinctions between each of these) and 'character' (however defined) are held in common. While dialogue is part of the armoury of novelistic devices, it takes on quite a different, and major, status in the drama. This, along with drama's relationship to performance, means that the manifestation and realisation of any common fictional principles in the writing process are very different.

Additionally, the how-to books reveal notions which owe allegiance to traditions of literary criticism derived from the novel, to some of the tenets of creative writing pedagogy and to theatre 'theory', reaching back to Aristotle. Indeed, there are some who still assert that Aristotle's principles are the guiding spirit behind today's mass medium of film, as if to argue that there are eternal, universal 'rules' for drama. As we shall see, matters are not so simple.

Linda Cowgill has claimed that Aristotle's dictates can simply be applied to screenwriting.[1] There is also the wonderfully titled *Aristotle's 'Poetics' for Screenwriters: Storytelling Secrets from the Greatest Mind in Western Civilisation*, by Michael Tierno. In 1949 the second edition of John Howard Lawson's book, *Theory and Technique of Playwriting* (first published in 1936), appeared. Expanding the book later to include a second half devoted to film, Lawson commented that 'Contemporary theories of technique are still based to a remarkable degree on Aristotle's principles,[2] and that 'Aristotle is the Bible of playwriting technique'.[3]

Robert McKee took a more historical approach. While Aristotle considered story as primary and character as secondary in drama, McKee pointed out that these principles were reversed as the novel became dominant. Even though McKee asserted that the argument about the primacy either of story or character is specious, he himself still privileged character: 'The revelation of true character . . . is fundamental to all fine storytelling.'[4] McKee also offered a structural estimate of the number of 'events', relative to different genres: a film may have between forty and sixty, a novel more than sixty and a play fewer than forty. Of course, this

---

[1] *Secrets of Screenplay Structure* (Lone Eagle, 1999), Hyperion, 2002.
[2] Ibid., p. 1.
[3] Ibid., p. 9.
[4] *Story*, p. 103.

all hinges on what one means by 'events'. In general terms, however, this is consonant with the fewer number of words the dramatist has at his/her disposal and the differentiated implications in terms of structure.

The following summaries come from a wide range of how-to-write-drama books: *The Crafty Art of Playmaking* by Alan Ayckbourn; *Dramatic Technique* by George Pierce Baker; *New Playwriting Strategies* by Paul Castagno; *The Sound of One Hand Clapping* by Sheila Yeger; *Stage Writing* by Val Taylor; *The Playwright's Guidebook* by Stuart Spencer; *Playwriting* by Sam Smily; *True and False* by David Mamet; *Three Uses of the Knife* by David Mamet; *Theory and Technique of Playwriting* by John Howard Lawson; *The Playwright's Workbook* by Jean-Claude van Italie; *Playwriting* by Noel Greig; *Writing a Play* by Steve Gooch; *The Art of Dramatic Writing* by Lajos Egri; *The Playwright's Handbook* by Frank Pike and Thomas G. Dunn.[5]

Each of the following sections reveals differences of opinion and contradictions, a great deal of serious commitment and often a singular lack of argued clarity in the books. Of course, this can be celebrated as diversity and variety, but it also testifies to the complexity and, at times, muddle in argued understandings of what constitutes the art of writing drama.

Action or character?

There are differing views on, and sometimes a conflation between, whether action or character is the prime determinant of drama. This is not a new debate and seems no nearer to being clearly understood or resolved, because the terms are never really defined. The issue

[5] Faber, 2002; Da Capo, 1976; Routledge, 2001; Amber Lane Press, 1990; Crowood Press, 2002; Faber, 2002; Yale University Press, 2005; Vintage, 1999; Vintage, 2000; Putnam's, 1949; Applause, 1997; Routledge, 2005; A & C Black, 2004; Isaac Pitman, 1950; Plume, Penguin, NY, 1996.

takes a particularly vexed form because of the concomitant of performance, where the concept of 'action' carries the empirical reality of three-dimensional physical movement.

Baker, Lawson, Pike and Gooch argue that 'action' is the more significant, 'character' is argued as primary by Archer and Smily. Most how-to books agree that drama generally has a 'protagonist', or, in Aristotelian terms, a 'hero', a single central character. Finally, in almost every one of the books discussed, *dialogue* only appears in one of the last chapters (if not *the* last), almost as an afterthought. Sometimes it is actively warned against as a dangerous device or activity, which might get in the way of the 'real' thing. This argument is often presented for methodological reasons – on the grounds that other kinds of preparation are necessary before the dialogue itself comes to be written. By implication this resonates with the form of the novel in which, indeed, dialogue is secondary.

This curious state of affairs is evidence of a conceptual problem in coming to terms with the distinctiveness of dramatic writing and a tendency (subliminal, conscious or not) to bring its principles in line with those of the novel.

Action, conflict and crisis (actions speak louder than words)

In criticism and theory of the novel, terms such as story or narrative or plot are commonly used. Indeed, literary theory has developed a strand of thought called narratology, which theorises the nature of narrative itself, as well as providing models of stories – fairy tales and myth are often cited as exemplars. In discussing drama, terms such as 'action', 'conflict', 'crisis' become the norm, eliding into concerns about character and ways in which 'character' and 'action' inter-relate. As we shall see, references to the imperatives of performance – onstage and in rehearsal – also influence the ways in which these issues are formulated in the books.

Lawson's inclusive definition owes as much to what happens in performance as it does to the conceptual work of the dramatist: 'Dramatic action is activity combining physical movement and speech; it includes the expectation, preparation and accomplishment of a change of equilibrium which is part of a series of such changes.'[6] A more specific definition of action for him is: 'Any change of equilibrium constitutes *an action*.'[7] In other words, an 'action' is a sequential moment in the narrative (story, plot).

In drama the particular narrative imperative is characterised as 'conflict'. According to Pike and Dunn, conflict is 'struggle, clash. Controversy, disagreement, opposition, collision, fight.'[8] Lawson pinpoints the nature of the conflict and its representation: 'The essential character of drama is social conflict – persons against other persons, or individuals against groups, or groups against other groups, or individuals or groups against social or natural forces – in which conscious will, exerted for the accomplishment of specific and understandable aims, is sufficiently strong to bring the conflict to a point of crisis.'[9]

The concept of crisis, a central, or most significant narrative moment, is considered essential: 'Crisis: a state of things in which a decisive change one way or the other is impending.'[10] Gooch stresses the importance in terms of 'a climax to the central bone of contention within the play, a moment where the clash of forces within it is at its keenest . . .'[11] The climax, or central narrative moment, then leads to 'the unknotting or disentangling of a complication' – what we might also call the denouement.[12] This narrative arc is then generally presented as the structure within which the drama is/must be written.

[6] Lawson, p. 173.
[7] Ibid., p. 171.
[8] Pike and Dunn, p. 33.
[9] Ibid., p. 168.
[10] Egri, p. 224.
[11] Gooch, p. 25.
[12] Archer, p. 192.

The theoretical justification for this structural notion of conflict and crisis is largely seen as mimetic: 'The plain truth seems to be that conflict is *one* of the most dramatic elements in life, and that many dramas . . . turn upon strife of one sort or another.'[13] Drama is thus seen as an imitation of 'life' (however that may be defined) in ways which, as we shall see later, have resonances with some of the ideas informing creative writing pedagogy.

However, the notion of 'action' as a driving force becomes either conflated with 'character' or with action as a means to an end: 'As a play dramatises a pattern of action it simultaneously explores human character. Drama, then, reveals the relationship of character to action . . .'[14] In the discussion about whether action or character 'drives' a play, there are some decisive claims: 'plays, strictly speaking, do not have actions. Characters do . . . Trying to talk about the action of a play is not real. Talking about a character is.'[15] Spencer is emphatic that 'Characters, in fact, drive every play that ever was'.[16] Gooch counters with the argument that 'action is the principal definer of character in a play.'[17]

Somewhere between these two positions, Ayckbourn argues: 'Characters in plays are there . . . to further the plot, whilst also informing us – directly or indirectly, through word or deed – of their individual thoughts and emotions.'[18]

[13] Ibid., p. 18.
[14] Smily, p. 123.
[15] Spencer, p. 42.
[16] Ibid., p. 210.
[17] Gooch, p. 72.
[18] Ayckbourn, p. 35.

Character

Whichever the prime mover may be (action or character), attempts to come to terms with the latter are equally diverse, even contradictory. First, following the mimetic line of argument, there are those who see characters as 'real' people. Taking his point of departure that character creates plot, Egri comments: 'You may not believe it, but the characters in a play are supposed to be real people. They are supposed to do things for reasons of their own.'[19] Using a more familiar formulation, Yeger argues: 'Creating believable characters . . . is perhaps the most important aspect of writing a play.'[20] The often repeated mantra that characters are or are not 'believable' or 'convincing' or 'real' permeates a great deal of dramatic criticism and is, in my experience, a mainstay of student response to drama.

But what exactly does it mean to suggest that a character must be convincing or believable? Attempts to provide guidance tend often to produce another familiar cliché or aphorism, that characters must/should be 'three-dimensional', or 'fully rounded' – whatever that may mean. This is often taken to be at the heart of the dramatist's task: 'Creating vivid, three-dimensional characters with a life of their own is probably the greatest challenge a new play-wright faces.'[21]

The relationship between the fictional/invented and the 'real' is at the core of this knotty formulation. An attempt to reconcile these different discourses informs one definition: 'Characters, however, are not human beings; they are constructions that resemble real people . . . In order to create lifelike characters, writers need to understand real people and apply their insights to their dramatic creations.'[22] In turn, this leads to the familiar advice to the dramatist

---

[19] Egri, p. 18.
[20] Yeger, p. 61.
[21] Pike and Dunn, p. 17.
[22] Smily, pp. 123–4.

to 'know the character as thoroughly as possible'.[23] And Ayckbourn clinches this with the claim: 'You can never know too much about your characters before you start.'[24] The concept of 'knowing' here stands in for the imagination and, according to the dominant principles in virtually all these books, this returns us to the impossible-to-define idea that 'characters' must, in some way, 'imitate' or be based on 'real life'.

Some observations wrestle with the problems raised by these simplistic mimetic assumptions: 'If characters in plays are not real people but inhabitants of that separate world within the author's head, by what criterion can they be judged effective?'[25] With a more conceptual approach to the significance of 'character', Taylor suggests: 'Stage characters are highly developed embodiments of . . . status distinctions.'[26] From this perspective, Gooch offers the more abstract view of 'characters as forces'.[27]

The difficulty of separating action from character has a material justification, because of the way human agency is foregrounded in dramatic writing, which consists of many, rather than a singular narrative voice, followed by and/or related to physical embodiment in performance. The crude mimetic notion that characters are somehow the same as or similar to people in real life leads to the semi-mystical notion that the characters somehow take control of the writing: 'Characters – central and secondary alike – must be allowed to write themselves . . . set them free to behave as they will.'[28]

[23] Egri, p. 32.
[24] Ayckbourn, p. 45.
[25] Gooch, p. 66.
[26] Taylor, p. 3.
[27] Gooch, p. 86.
[28] Spencer, p. 190.

Premise, idea, vision, theme

While discussions of action and character constantly revert to discussions of mimesis and real life, at the other extreme is a concern with an issue which seems to be more particular to drama than to other fictional forms. All the books wrestle with this; the terms are often interchangeable and the exhortations are grand, if not apocalyptic. A play apparently must have 'a well formulated premise'[29] and Ayckbourn warns: 'Never start a play without an idea.'[30] Ultimately, argues Gooch, 'A play's idea is, after all, the most important thing in it.'[31]

This 'idea' seems to be associated with a theme, or a message, something the author needs or wants to 'say': 'Your theme is what you want to say in your play.'[32] Gooch defines this as 'a sense of the world',[33] while Pike and Dunn prefer the term 'vision', ominously suggesting that 'Defining your vision takes time, perhaps a lifetime'.[34]

The difficulty with all these is that, however serious and well-meaning the attempts are, major questions of theme and imaginative execution are at stake. Critical literature is packed with competing argued exegeses of what the most important idea, premise, theme of any work of literature (novel, poem or drama) may be. To expect or assume, let alone to demand, that dramatists must be able to provide their own cut-and-dried critical understanding of the play they have not yet written is fairly odd, to say the least. Of course it is important to *think*; but the relationships between thinking, imagining and writing drama are infinitely more complex than these exhortations suggest.

[29] Egri, p. 6.
[30] Ayckbourn, p. 6.
[31] Gooch, p. 7.
[32] Spencer, p. 154.
[33] Gooch, p. 24.
[34] Pike and Dunn, p. 88.

Scenario

The demand for the dramatist to be able to 'know' and, presumably, articulate his or her idea or premise or theme at the start, also permeates approaches to methodology and the process of writing itself. Virtually all the books suggest starting with a scenario. Ayckbourn summarises the process, based on his own way of working as writer and director: 'Preparatory work is vital to all playmaking . . . The questions need to be asked: how, when, where and with whom are you going to choose to tell your story? In other words, *narrative, time, location, characters*.'[35]

More concrete advice entails writing a complete scenario, listing scenes, with information about what happens in each scene: 'it's really valuable to spend substantial time planning the complete arc of your story from beginning to end, before you actually start to write the scenes.'[36] While there is nothing wrong in principle with beginning with an outline/scenario/plan, there is a very serious problem heralded by the implication of this kind of preparation. This may stem from privileging action over character: 'Thinking through the play means . . . perfecting what the characters do before worrying about what they say.'[37] But there is significant censorship involved.

Dialogue

The censorship imposed is on the very fabric of writing drama itself, the production of dialogue. It begins with a health warning: 'You have probably spent a long time creating the detailed scenario. You're probably aching to start writing dialogue. Not yet. Take a break.'[38]

[35] Ayckbourn, p. 12.
[36] Taylor, p. 67.
[37] Smily, p. 37.
[38] Pike and Dunn, p. 113.

Breathtakingly, dialogue is addressed only in the last part of the how-to books, then sparingly treated, with the student advised to leave dialogue till last. Archer, Lawson, Smily, Spencer and Taylor refer to dialogue only in the last twenty pages or so of their books, Egri about ten pages from the end.

Ayckbourn argues that everything should be planned in detail – a process which should take about a year – before any dialogue is written. McKee, writing about film scripts, advises: 'The wise writer puts off the writing of dialogue for as long as possible, because *the premature writing of dialogue chokes creativity.*'[39]

Locking into the argument that action is more important than character, Gooch advises: 'To think in terms of an "action", then, of what *happens* on the stage, is far more important to a playwright than the dialogue.'[40] Picking up the line that character is more important, Smily comments that 'Thoughts in characters within plots must exist before words can be put on paper',[41] though quite how and where they 'exist' is not at all clear.

Dialogue in itself can be diminished or denigrated if it appears too soon, 'The characters talk, but nothing much happens'[42] and 'writing dialogue can be very similar to an actor performing an improvisation'.[43] At the other end of the spectrum, and even though he gives only four pages to dialogue towards the end of his book, Spencer does acknowledge that 'it is the one, solitary means by which you have to express everything you have to say: theme, character, story, plot.'[44]

We are faced with the paradox that dialogue appears to be both the last and least important part of the process (or impossible to write until everything else has been decided), and that it is the most significant part of the manifestations of dramatic writing.

[39] McKee, p. 417.
[40] Gooch, p. 23.
[41] Smily, p. 183.
[42] Ibid., p. 35.
[43] Gooch, p. 60.
[44] Spencer, p. 195.

Narrative and causality

The stress on scenario and planning, taken apart from its censorship of dialogue, does, however, address the important issue of structure. As has been pointed out, there is generally more fluidity in the way chapters operate in novels than there is in the way scenes operate as building blocks of the structure of drama. In drama, as a general principle, changes in time and place are marked by new scenes. The notion of action returns here to lend shape to the greater foregrounding of cause-and-effect relations in drama and dramatic plotting.

McKee argues that the drama begins with the 'inciting incident', and Taylor rounds up the totality of the structure: 'cause and effect sequences as units of action help to generate the movement we require to bring about change.'[45] Cause and effect are enacted through a more clearly conceptualised formulation of ordering: '*Sequence* means a continuous and connected series, a succession of repetitions, or a set of ordered elements. It implies order, continuity, progressions. An *event* refers to an occurrence of importance that has an antecedent cause, a consequent result, or both.'[46] It is worth noting that all of this could equally well apply to the structuring of a novel.

Drama and creative writing

The contexts in which drama is currently taught derive from the dominant practice of teaching creative writing in the workshop. This returns us in a rather different way to the concept of drama as mimesis, as imitation – in this case, of the dramatist's personal 'experiences' or life. The idea of writing 'what you know' is a common one in creative writing pedagogy and clearly it has real

[45] Taylor, p. 58.
[46] Smily, p. 101.

resonance; many writers of all kinds may draw on aspects of their experiences and memories. However, when this is elevated to a writerly principle it becomes restrictive and problematic: 'The major source for writers is *direct experience*.'[47] At the very least, this imposes a serious limitation on the dramatist's imagination – unless, of course, we assume that Shakespeare knew what it was to be a king and/or a murderer. More cosily, we are enjoined: 'Just think of your aunt Helen, the family gossip.'[48]

As was argued in chapter 6, one of the double-binds of creative writing pedagogy is the simultaneous promise (explicit or implicit) that a course will enable the student to become a professional writer, along with a series of warnings. This results in a paradoxical construct: talent versus creativity. Egri claims that we all have creative ability, while at the same time cautioning that 'Even if you will never be a genius, your enjoyment of life can still be great.'[49]

If you are lucky enough to be able to fight off the fear that you may not be a genius, 'merely' creative, there are further problems: Writing a play entails entering 'a bustling and terrifying arena',[50] in which 'it's really normal to be frightened.'[51] From this follows all the usual assumptions that if you have no exciting or worthy experiences about which to write, you will end up with writer's block; and if you have no talent (the implicit *sine qua non* of creative writing), then the very purpose of all pedagogy – the assumption that there is something to teach and something to learn – is rendered superfluous. You either have it or you don't have it.

[47] Smily, p. 12.
[48] Egri, p. ix.
[49] Ibid., p. xii.
[50] Yeger, p. 18.
[51] Ibid., p. 12.

Conclusions – dialogue – the absent centre

All the books from which I have quoted were written by know-ledgeable and experienced practitioners, committed to thinking about what is entailed in writing drama. They rely heavily on aphorisms and often contradictory definitions. Clearly any student or teacher could easily take from these the bits they like or agree with, or which appeal to them as newly enlightening sayings. But, with all due respect to the commitment of their authors, none of the books go very far beyond definitions, assertions and tips. While they may challenge their reader/users to think, they tend to provide prescriptive advice and one book often contradicts another. The relatively common-sense critical notions often owe unacknowledged allegiance to ideas derived from the novel, with little far-reaching investigation into the genre of drama, its distinctiveness and what is at stake in developing skills in the art of writing drama.

Particularly telling is the virtual exclusion of the central textual element in drama which is contained in dialogue. At best the books are evasive, at worst they mostly dismiss the importance of dialogue. Images of babies and bathwater spring to mind. There are two exceptions to the list from which I have culled examples – *The Playwright's Workbook* by Jean-Claude van Italie[52] and *Playwriting: a practical guide* by Noel Greig,[53] both of which address the writing of dialogue in a concrete, and to some extent, cumulative way. In particular, Greig's book is a meticulous and gently detailed progressive work which first initiates students into 'creative writing' in a generic fashion, before spelling out stage by stage exercises which introduce students to the practicalities of putting dialogue on the page. However, even in this very useful text, the writing of dialogue rests on many of the unquestioned principles and clichés which have been discussed in this book. A different, more genre-specific approach is very much needed.

[52] Applause, 1997.
[53] Routledge, 2005.

8   Stage directions

Following the brief discussion about narrative voice in chapter 5, it may seem that stage directions provide a bridge between the novel and the drama. After all, they are generally written in prose, and they are a distinctive, specialised form of 'narration', 'description', or 'direction' in an impersonal voice. The voicing of stage directions is not within the mono-vocality of any individual character; it is 'outside' the action, generally written in the third person. While drama-writing manuals may spend some pages discussing the importance of location or setting, very little space is generally given to stage directions. Such discussions are also relatively rare in theatre theory – Aston and Savona rightly comment that stage directions are 'a particularly undeveloped topic'.[1]

Where stage directions *are* discussed, they are implicitly or explicitly compared with the novel. In the drama such description may be seen as second-best, as Baker wrote: 'Let it be remembered . . . that the stage direction is not a pocket into which a dramatist may stuff whatever explanation, description, or analysis a novelist might allow himself, but is more a last resort to which he turns when he cannot make his text convey all that is necessary.'[2] From this angle, stage directions are secondary parts of the written text,

[1] Aston and Savona, op. cit., p. 71.
[2] Baker, op. cit., p. 279.

because they compensate for something the dramatist has been unable to do (*pace* Baker), or because they are truncated versions of something the novel can do better; or something which, more fully written, belongs in a novel: this is all an extension of the 'incomplete' status generally attributed to the dramatic text. In any case, stage directions can never compete with their equivalents in the novel. As Martin Esslin wrote, 'verbal accounts of the visuals lack the evocative power descriptive passages hold in narrative literature.'[3]

The inadequacy of such description, compared with its potential adequacy in the novel, has been reinforced by some critics. Raymond Williams suggested that stage directions indirectly perform a function which is more explicit in prose fiction: 'Much of the detailed description of atmosphere, character, look, gesture and manner of speech comes in fact from another literary form, the novel, in which this kind of description can be direct.'[4] To clinch the argument that stage directions are either indirect or incomplete in comparison with the novel, he makes the salutary point that if Chekhov had spelled everything out, he would have ended up writing a novel.

Main or subsidiary

Aston and Savona have argued for stage directions and dialogue to be seen as integral parts of the same (if ambiguous, 'incomplete', in their terms) text. They take as their guideline theorist Roman Ingarden's distinction between the dialogue as '*Haupttext*' (main text) and stage directions as '*Nebentext*' (subsidiary, marginal text). The fact that such a distinction is necessary at all again refers outwards to, on the one hand, the novel, and on the other to the processes of production/performance.

[3] *The Field of Drama*, p. 81.
[4] *Drama in Performance*, p. 129.

Acknowledging 'the status of the novel as the dominant literary form of the modern period', Aston and Savona have attempted to heal the breach between the two textual elements: 'it is hardly surprising that the play-text is often read as a novel manqué',[5] by suggesting ways in which to follow Ingarden and see 'stage directions and dialogue . . . as complementary and interdependent signifying systems'.[6]

This appears to be supported by Patrice Pavis: 'For the text itself, notation traditionally takes the form of linguistic transcription, with its own methods suitable for indicating change of speaker and the author's or director's stage directions. But as soon as one wishes to describe the unfolding of a concrete production, the system of notation must take account of an unlimited ensemble which can cover visual and acoustic phenomena expressed by means of stage systems.'[7] Aston and Savona rely on stage directions as the written signifier of an active connection between written text and performance: 'the implication that the dual identity of the dramatic text, its simultaneous existence as literary artefact and as blueprint for production, may be argued with regard to the stage directions – the guarantors, as it were, of the text's theatrical potential – themselves.'[8]

There is no real sense in which the stage directions actually do or can guarantee the text's 'theatrical potential', since, as we shall see, stage directions and dialogue generate different kinds of ambiguity in relation to performance. Additionally, whatever their complete/ incomplete status, stage directions can always be read as part of a distinctive kind of written text in its own right – i.e., they are 'read' as prose, rather than dialogue. While the form of the novel allows for an integration between two different modes of writing (prose/

---

[5] Aston and Savona, op. cit., p. 72.
[6] Ibid., p. 73.
[7] Patrice Pavis, *Language of the Stage* (Performing Arts Journal Publications, 1993), p. 113.
[8] Aston and Savona, op. cit., p. 75.

dialogue), the form of the drama, both on the page and in performance, does not operate so seamlessly.

From directions to performance

Aston and Savona assume a linear progression between text and performance: 'the reading of a performance action *from the text* is a logical and straightforward proceeding.'[9] In fact, it is anything but. They indirectly acknowledge this by suggesting that some stage directions are addressed to the performer, and that 'the directions which are relevant to the work of the designer, the lighting designer and the technician may be regarded as constituting an outline brief'.[10] As we shall see later, there is a qualitative difference between the addressees (literal) of dialogue and stage directions (putative).

The reality is that one can, and should, take stage directions as an entirely different kind of guarantor: of redundancy. As soon as the dramatic text goes anywhere near the production process, one can guarantee that the stage directions will – effectively, because they must – go out of the window and be ignored. Dialogue, on the other hand, can never be jettisoned; it must be explored, reproduced and transformed from written to spoken form.

Aston and Savona's book does, however, provide some fascinating categorisation of stage directions, with implications for writing dialogue. Dividing them into the 'intra-dialogic' and the 'extra-dialogic', they make a distinction, which, for the purposes of this book (see later in this chapter) draws attention to the indicators *from within the dialogue itself* that some 'action' has happened. The categories include elements which apply to character identification, facts about appearance, information about voice and facial expression. This is an interesting exercise and is well worth reading.

[9] Ibid., p. 76.
[10] Ibid., p. 133.

However, it may help to compound the ambiguities attached to stage directions, rather than clarify what they are, what they cannot be and what relevance they may or may not have for the dramatist as writer.

Aston and Savona are not the only ones to assume a straight line from stage directions to performance. Where stage directions have been addressed in the how-to books, authors take a similar approach. Val Taylor suggested that they are instructions 'to a member of the team . . . try to think of them as invitations'.[11] Adrian Page actually seemed to believe that through stage directions (*Nebentext*) 'a playwright can ordain exactly how the dialogue is to be played and what effects should derive from it'.[12]

Directors must, of course, 'interpret' stage directions – or not. Director David Jones, working with film, has offered a comment which can, effectively, also stand for directors' attitudes to stage directions: 'with a movie script it is much more difficult to strike a balance between the writer's concept and the continual nudge towards how the thing might be directed.'[13] The scripts he read in Hollywood were 'horribly full of directorial comments, which I don't think should be there . . . they not only tell *you* at great length what every character is feeling at every moment . . . but also they tell you what you are feeling about what the character's feeling . . . What I want is the events, the characters and what they say, then there's a mystery left in the story and I have a job to do.'[14]

Two material arguments gainsay the idea that stage directions are genuine, workable instructions to the various skills involved in production, and that they lead straight to performance. This is connected with the argument that there are different systems of signification operating in writing and performance. In the case of dialogue the language moves from written to spoken or enunciated

[11] Taylor, op. cit., p. 118.
[12] *The Death of the Playwright* edited by Adrian Page (Macmillan, 1992), p. 6.
[13] Jones and Nelson, op. cit., p. 48.
[14] Ibid., p. 49.

form. The word 'fish' on the page will recognisably sound as 'fish', although *how* it is said/inflected is subject to what we call 'interpretation', which depends on narrative context and purpose. In the case of stage directions, the written form becomes redundant in principle. In practice, while it may be a pleasantly suggestive part of reading the text-on-the-page, it can never be precisely matched or correlated with what is visualised, or non-linguistically represented.

There is an assumption, by analogy with the conventions of the post-classical musical score, that dynamics and expression markings are the equivalent of stage directions; that is, they are instructions for performance. This is only partially the case. Metronome markings, which define the duration of a particular 'length' note, can be included, to give a precise guideline for the basic pulse of a piece or movement in a piece. So, for example, a crotchet = 85 can be precisely set on the metronome and the pulse followed by performers. However, in practice, this is likely to vary (deliberately, or by chance); it might be above or below 85; it might, according to the aesthetic vagaries of conductor or performer, be speeded up to 100, or slowed down to 60. The 85 is a technical approximation, which in performance is more likely to refer to gradations of speed between different sorts of 'fast' and different sorts of 'slow'.

What does not, however, allow of variety is the fact that all the notes of the piece are very carefully demarcated relative to the dominant pulse or note value. The move from written to aural (the sounded) can be precisely correlated; that is, a note in the appropriate place on the stave indicates a 'C' at a certain pitch. However, even this is historically variable. Our current reference point, that the sound of an A = 440, works for classical and modern music, but anything written before (say) the middle of the eighteenth century might well have been played at one of a number of slightly lower pitches. The early music movement has extensively explored such historical documentation, with the result that the same marking on a stave (say, our middle C) can sound at one of a number of possible (all aurally quite close together) pitches. In

Renaissance music, in any case, such markings were virtually entirely absent; it is not until the era of Classical music and after (the full era of public staging of both concerts and theatre) that such additional musical 'stage directions' arrived.

Historical studies of stage directions in drama confirm this variability and instability. There is very little documentation of the way plays were actually staged between the 1580s and early 1640s. The editors of *A Dictionary of Stage Directions in English Drama 1580–1642* collected over 22,000 examples of stage directions.[15] There is no certainty about whether or how these were or might have been observed in performance, nor about who actually wrote them down: dramatist, stage manager, scribe? There is also no way of knowing whether the directions were written in before or after the first or subsequent performances.

It is often the same with published plays today. Stage directions might just as easily be a notated record of what happened in the first production and included by the dramatist, rather than what the dramatist wrote as part of his/her 'own' text. Of course, in a sense this is a testament to the contribution of 'teamwork' to the written text, post hoc. If the dramatist doesn't like what the director did, because she/he owns the copyright to the written and published text, she/he may change it at will, and there will be no record of the director's work on the page.

The plays published by Samuel French for the amateur market make a point of including fairly detailed drawings of the possible stage settings, and lists of props and costumes, to help guide the amateur production process. These are more likely to come from the play's first production, rather than from the pen of the dramatist. The same may, of course, apply to any changes to the dialogue during rehearsal of the first production of a new play; changes approved by the dramatist may appear in the published text, or they may be ignored, as the author returns to his/her

[15] Alan C. Dessen and Leslie Thomson (Cambridge University Press, 2000). First published 1999.

preferred version.

Extra-dialogic stage directions

Customarily, a written drama will begin with some indication of its setting, its time and/or the characters who first appear on stage. The following quotations are examples to support my arguments. Anyone interested in the changes in stage directions through the twentieth century should take a selection of drama from different decades, to see how the practice has been changing. Generally speaking, as the twentieth century progressed, stage directions became more sparse. This is partly to do with some of the post-1968 explorations of more open styles of staging, away from the 'traditional' proscenium arch.

These are the opening words of three plays, all stage directions, written over the span of nearly a century. They are offered for analysis, not as lessons for how to write stage directions, or as examples of what to avoid:

> '*A pleasant room, tastefully, but not expensively furnished.*' (*A Doll's House*, Henrik Ibsen, first published 1879.)
> '*A fine spring morning on the river Meuse, between Lorraine and Champagne, in the year 1429, A.D., in the castle of Vaucouleurs.*' (*Saint Joan*, George Bernard Shaw, first published 1924.)
> '*The Porters' one-room flat in a large Midland town.*' (*Look Back in Anger*, John Osborne, first published 1957.)

As opening sentences, they have a number of things in common: first of all, none of the sentences has a verb. Each is couched in a declamatory style, like announcements. The first and third describe an interior location (room, flat), the second a more general geographical location and the time of day. Ibsen indicates the class orientation of the room's owners and his sentence could be read as implicitly addressed primarily to the set designer. Shaw creates a novel-like cultural setting, which also pinpoints the historical distance of the action flagging the fact that this is a history play. Osborne's is the only opening to mention any people – the Porters – and it implicitly assumes that the reader is likely to be English and will understand the oblique reference to the '*Midlands*'. All three sentences, in their different ways, could be implied as addressed most directly to the set designer. If they appeared as the beginnings to novels, they would be 'read' as stylistically unusual, quirky even, in relation to conventional prose-based expectations.

On further examination, all the opening stage-direction sentences turn out to be little more than the most basic and general of 'instructions', rather than information which can be literally translated into a performance text. What is '*pleasant*', '*tastefully*', '*not expensively*'? What does a '*fine spring morning*' look like? How 'large' is the town? How is it to be indicated, if at all? Is it background information, or visual clue? Interpretation, interpretation, interpretation. Interpretation inevitably opens up the possibility of deviation.

The declamatory openings signify the dramatic convention of the here-and-nowness, the present continuousness of the stage moment/performance. This is ironically reinforced by the absence of a verb and therefore by the absence of any tense referring to either an identifiable past or an identifiable present. Performance, with the audience there, always takes place within the demarcated space and time of the 'performed', continuous present. As with poetry, which more conventionally and acceptably dispenses with verbs, we read the opening sentences as taking place in an abstract present. We thus read informed by a number of conventions in mind: those of performance, poetry, drama and prose.

After the opening announcements, the prose settles into more sequential paragraphs. The stage directions at the beginning of *Look Back in Anger* consist of three substantial paragraphs. The first is 'addressed' to the structural controllers – the designer and the set builders: '*The ceiling slopes down quite sharply from L to R.*' There is a generalised list of furniture: '*a heavy chest of drawers*' – but what colour, how large, who decides whether it is 'heavy', and is 'heavy' to be somehow visible, detectable? The paragraph is written in the third person, in the present tense. The directional indicators, 'L' and 'R' (Left and Right), are theatrical shorthand, suggesting that the narrator has some relationship to them from wherever she/he is positioned. By analogy with the lack of verbs in the opening sentences, this device also flouts the conventions of prose.

Since the 'scene' is what is (implicitly) onstage, this might suggest that the narrator is on the stage, and that L and R are to his/her L and R. However, the next paragraph changes the perspective. The first sentence, '*At rise of curtain,* JIMMY *and* CLIFF *are seated in the two armchairs R L respectively*' suggests that they cannot be seen *until* the rise of the curtain, i.e., it is only then that they can be seen from the front of the stage. The next sentence confirms this, pluralising the narrative voice: '*All that we can see . . .*'. The narrative voice is now 'in' the (plural, 'we') audience, as it were: '*At rise of curtain*' (note the shorthand again, no definite articles), and then, if the narrative voices are now positioned in the audience, R and L are reversed. That is, the audience's 'right' is actually the 'left' of anyone standing onstage. The sentence contains two narrative vantage points simultaneously, before jumping off the stage and settling in the auditorium.

In the second paragraph we home in on Jimmy and Cliff in more detail, with the narrative voice occasionally reversing its vantage point, to 'jump' back behind the action, moving from first person plural to third person singular. So '*we* find' that Jimmy '*is a tall, thin young man about twenty-five, wearing a very worn tweed jacket and flannels*'. But then we are 'told' with certainty that he '*is a disconcerting mixture of sincerity . . .*' etc. He and Cliff are described in terms of their physical appearance (Cliff is '*short, dark, big boned*') and their contrasting personality traits, in an authoritative third-person narrative voice.

The point has already been made about the generalised 'instructions' to set designer and props manager, or set builders. The same is now true for costume: what is a 'very worn' tweed jacket? What colour(s) is it? What sort of flannels? Grey? What kind of grey? What is he wearing under the jacket? On his feet? What colour are his socks? What happens if the best actor to audition is thirty-five, not that tall and not that thin? What assumptions do we conventionally make about what twenty-five 'looks' like?

Even the description of Jimmy's personality, presented by the narrator, as either *'sensitive to the point of vulgarity'*, *'simply a loudmouth'*, or *'almost non-committal'*, do not necessarily cohere. Clearly, these are post hoc 'interpretations' of a persona, made by someone who already knows about him and his social context. 'We', the audience, are not in that privileged position, since the play has not yet begun. If the 'instructions' can also be seen as addressed to the actor about to play Jimmy, there are no specific clues about how the traits described are to be projected into the performance. In any case, during the course of rehearsal an interpretive decision might be made that he is not simply a loudmouth, or that he is neither sensitive nor vulgar, but possible just a sadist. I am not arguing that this is a right or better interpretation, just that it is possible and that such possibilities might produce very different sets of character 'motivation' from the ones in the stage directions, while absolutely adhering to exactly the same dialogue.

The third paragraph returns to the third person singular narrator. Alison is now the subject of this paragraph but, unlike with the men, the vocabulary about her is metaphorical, rather than psychological, resorting to musical metaphor: in *'the uneasy polyphony of these three people'*, Alison is *'tuned in a different key'*, *'often drowned in the robust orchestration . . .'*. The last four lines of this final paragraph pull out to the front of the auditorium again, describing the room, its sounds, returning full circle to the *'early evening'* of the opening direction. After this stylistic completion, the play's initial 'action' begins. Jimmy throws down his paper and the dialogue takes over.

Extra- and intra-dialogic stage directions

On the first full page of dialogue in *Look Back in Anger* there are three further kinds of stage direction:

> JIMMY Well, you *are* ignorant. You're just a peasant. (*To Alison.*) What about you? You're not a peasant, are you?
> ALISON (*absently*) What's that?
> JIMMY I said . . .

In the first speech Jimmy is responding to Cliff, telling him he is a peasant. He then asks someone else whether she/he is a peasant. Since Alison is the only other person onstage, it must be addressed to her. Whichever way Alison emotes the phrase 'What's that?' she is indicating (honestly or not) that she hasn't, apparently, heard the remark. Jimmy repeats what he said. While on the page, the presence of the stage direction increases the clarity of the change of addressee (we already know that there are three people onstage, so it isn't strictly necessary to clarify). However, as soon as the scene is read aloud or performed, it is entirely clear that there is a change of addressee.

Later on in the scene:

> JIMMY (*shouting*) All right, dear. Go back to sleep. It was only me talking . . .

The stage direction appears to be addressed to the actor playing Jimmy, about the level at which he might pitch his speech. Of course, aggression or frustration can be expressed in a number of different vocal ways: shouting is merely one option. If, during rehearsal, this line proves to be more 'effective' if it is not strictly 'shouted', then the spirit of the stage direction could be said to be observed, without interpreting it as a literal shout. Besides which, shouting is itself a vocal delivery of highly variable pitch. There are shouts and shouts.

Finally, the third kind of stage direction. After Jimmy says:

JIMMY   . . . She's educated. (*To her.*) That's right, isn't it?

Cliff replies:

CLIFF (*kicking out at him from behind his paper*)   Leave her alone, I said.

JIMMY   Do that again, you Welsh ruffian, and I'll pull your ears off.

A switching of addressee is signalled in the first speech (as before). In the next speech there is an instruction for physical action to the actor playing Cliff. Now, from Jimmy's retort – 'Do that again . . .' – we know that Cliff has 'done' something (i.e., this is an 'intra-dialogic' indication that something has happened. The action draws a strong response: 'I'll pull your ears off.' We know from (most important) both the dialogue and stage directions at the beginning (less important), that both men are reading newspapers. So the action *might* be newspaper-related but, clearly, it doesn't have to be.

At three different levels the stage directions, intra- and extra-dialogic, are unstable:

1. First, they are invariably narrated, here in the third person and first person plural. This signifies the presence of a 'character', a voice 'outside' the fiction proper. It is common, of course, to assume this is the 'author's' voice, simply because it is a set of instructions provided with a voice of putative authority from outside the fictional world. However, as we know, they could have been written by anyone at all: director, scribe, stage manager or a publisher's editor. The narrative voice is couched so as to represent someone who knows about the conventions of theatre and

performance, but the distinctive necessity of authorship predicated by the dialogue is – fundamentally – irrelevant for the stage directions. It is also a bracketed 'novelistic' device.

2. Intra-dialogic stage directions confirm that physical 'action' (to simplify, for the moment) will inevitably always be indicated, to some extent, from within the dialogue itself. A line leading up to what is written as a stage direction will always indicate, or prepare the ground for, the stage direction: Cliff's 'Leave her alone, I said' comes before Jimmy's (*shouting*) and a line of dialogue following a written direction will always indicate that something different or physical has just happened – in other words dialogue following physical action will (at some point) be a *reaction* to the physical action. This is because, as we shall see more clearly in chapter 10 on dialogue, every speech event or physical event is a *reaction* to what has gone before. It cannot be otherwise. In any case, Cliff also ripostes with 'Stop yelling', which is a much clearer indicator than *shouting* of the pitch of his voice. Although, even here, this could be ironic/sarcastic. Jimmy might whisper and Cliff might send him up by referring to it as 'yelling'. Again, I am not saying this is a right or better interpretation, just that it is possible, since forms of articulation and delivery onstage come within the purview of 'interpretation'.

3. Directional instructions (*to her*) which precede lines are there to ease the reading-on-the page process and directions on how to speak a word or line may be the right/best way, but they may well also not be. In any case all such directions within and between the dialogue are always – and must be – totally up for grabs during rehearsal and exploration.

In other words all stage directions on the page are inherently unstable. This is a polite, semi-academic way of saying that they are jettisoned and/or ignored as soon as any significant rehearsal process begins, because they are, from the point of view of production, ultimately and genuinely irrelevant and/or redundant. This is a drama, not a novel. To stand a chance of being relevant and convince anyone that they are/have been carried out, they would have to be part of a novel, where all the text has the same status in relation to readability – i.e., fixed at publication. The dialogue in a drama always remains fundamentally stable in a literal sense, even though its delivery/enunciation is not. The critical loyalty of director and performers is, and can only be, simply and entirely and literally, just to the dialogue.

4. The fourth level of instability is an extension of the relationship between written text and performed text, and that is the relationship between different signifying systems. Dialogue on the page continues to be the same 'language' to the letter in performance, but now heard rather than read, enunciated rather than written. The 'meanings', therefore, belong to different systems and to different material processes, which owe their effectiveness to different forms of transformative labour – reading, interpreting and realising, in the mind and onstage.

Conclusions

This chapter does not consist of a set of instructions about how to write stage directions. It does not lay down rules or guidelines about what stage directions must or must not be, or which ones other practitioners like best, which ones they ignore most readily and which ones they swear at. It argues that students need to understand the historical variability of stage directions and to be extremely sceptical about any idea that they are justified as 'instructions' to the production team. The best way of understanding this is through a mixture of direct experience of production, together with a study and analysis of the historical variability of stage directions.

From the point of view of the written text it is possible to characterise the mixture of dialogue and stage directions as constituting a dual identity, in which one part (directions) is always ambiguous (not always usefully so), while the other (dialogue) is not. However, even this does not go far enough. When considered from the point of view of the art and practice of writing, something more interesting emerges. While from a semiological point of view the two systems of signification (page and stage) clearly share the written text in common, from the student's point of view there is another writerly lesson to be learned. If a student becomes supremely interested in writing stage directions, imaginatively immersed in the detail of such writing, it may mean that his/her imaginative predilections are drawn more strongly to prose fiction than they are to drama. This is always worth considering seriously. A course in studying the art of writing drama could as easily lead to a student's discovery that this is not, after all, where his/her imaginative/writing skills lie. At least he/she will have understood why.

9 The compleat dramatist – preparing to write

The main argument throughout this book is that the process of creating (writing) a dramatic text is, from the point of view of the writer, complete in itself. This does not invalidate processes where there is devising or company workshopping, but the latter do not provide the necessary internalising of writing and performance conventions which each would-be dramatist must experience. It means that any drama-writing pedagogy must be approached from the perspective of its relatively autonomous status. This is not a return to the good old days when drama was simply studied on the page, to the exclusion of any understanding of the complexity of performance, and of the many ways in which meanings are created in the interface between writing and performance. It is an argument for stressing that the dramatist him/herself is in charge of the learning and writing process, however much he/she may learn about what performers and directors do.

Any course of study which addresses itself to the written dramatic text *still* must, in some form, treat the text as a literary artefact, of a very distinctive kind. Its specialness lies precisely in a relationship to production through performance, which is one of the distinguishing features of drama, in comparison with prose fiction and poetry. Indeed, until this can be fully recognised I suggest that the traditional dichotomy between what theatre studies 'does' with published texts and how the newer discipline of

Performance Studies analyses performance will be perpetuated.

At the same time the recognition that the dramatic text is always conceptually complete as a special kind of literary artefact makes it possible to free up critical and theoretical work to address it for what it is. The important issue here is that the dramatist is necessarily in charge at every point in the process. This applies from the submission of the first draft, the rewriting processes, the final decision about what goes into rehearsal and what is published.

Copyright

This corresponds, of course, to concepts of authorship which have been questioned and challenged by theory, but not overthrown or usurped by it. This is as much to do with the economic position of the dramatist as it is to do with any concepts of ideological purity. Copyright and ownership of a text mean that its author, over-whelmingly in an insecure freelance position in the artistic economy, is able to earn from further exploitation (sales) of the work. Any drama is as much a commodity as anything else in our capitalist economy (wrong or right, this is a fact). Further earnings mean royalties from sales of books, or from further productions, where the dramatist receives a royalty (percentage) of income from the theatre.

At the producing end of the process it is entirely accepted that, intertextuality notwithstanding (another important development in literary theory) individual authorship is always attributed. Each text, whichever conventions and traditions it belongs to, is a unique combination of elements – linguistic, conceptual, imaginative. Otherwise there would be literally no difference between one poem and another etc., etc.

The story so far

This book began by charting the different histories, cultural and educational, which have led to the prevalence of a number of clichés, the most overarching (and misleading) of which is that the dramatic text is incomplete. This disenfranchisement of text and dramatist has come from a number of directions, all ultimately damaging to any productive idea of exactly what it is that the dramatist does and what she/he produces. Each of these other perspectives suppresses the point of view of the dramatist and, indeed, subsumes issues involved with dramatic writing into issues appropriate to other practices. These include the practical business of production; the academic practice of performance and theatre studies; and the literary study of the novel.

On one side the imperatives of production and performance have diminished the dramatist and his/her responsibility towards the written text; on the other it has been seen as a novel manqué, lacking features intrinsic to the novel and thus making it impossible or, at best, difficult, to 'read'. Performance theory, with its exciting insights into understanding the sign systems which create meanings through visualisation and representation, has also directed attention away from the written text. For serious students of the art of writing drama, some in-depth study of all these is important, so that they can understand the ideas in relation to which their learning process takes place. At the same time an understanding of the exciting range of possibilities of dialogue in performance through some experience of acting is also critical.

From prose to dialogue

Part of the problem derives from the linguistic features of the dramatic text itself: the co-presence within it of 'narrated' prose (via stage directions) and of 'pure' dialogue, presented quite free (it is thought) of the surrounding contextualisation of the novel. Because of the necessary links with performance, assumptions that the dramatist somehow 'writes' or inscribes, or even is able to inscribe, the process of production within the written text itself has also confused matters.

For the purposes of the remainder of this book, there is one very obvious starting point. This is that writing drama is a distinctive form of the imaginative mode of thought, realised in and through dialogue alone. Not primarily and not alongside other ways of writing. Dialogue is all and dialogue is all there is. This is not to deny the relationship with performance, nor to deny shared elements with other forms of imaginative writing – prose and poetry. It is not even to deny that dramatists have included, and some might well continue to include, stage directions. They are, however, secondary, subsidiary, provisional and a compensatory element.

The basic and ongoing continuing process of transforming imagined material from the mind/brain to the page in the form of the dramatic text means that everything must, in the end, be sustained by the dialogue. Although it is the case that there is much less dialogue in a film than there is in a stage play, in the end the same principle applies. No film script is ever accepted and produced on the basis of its 'stage directions', its visuals. While it may be structured according to cinematic formulae, conventionally judged elements of story, characters, action and conflict etc. are what clinch the deal.

Narrative through dialogue

The dramatic text is a narrative told through the convention or literary device of dialogue. It is highly formalised – each speaker's name stands at the left-hand side of the page – all that really remains in the body of the text of impersonal narrative. This is just for ease of reading – in performance the dialogue remains, but there is no need for someone to come and name each 'character' before he/she 'speaks'. The written is transformed in production to the enunciated. This is only one of the ways in which the text can be read. It can also be read perfectly well on the page, complete in itself.

Monologue and character

The embodiment of drama in the performer (the human agent) seems to lend particular significance to the concept of 'character'; the words-on-the-page representation of a human figure is given 'life' in the three-dimensional appearance of the performer. This is part of the rationale behind the still powerful Aristotelian concept that drama is 'about' a single hero (or heroine). In fact, as we shall see, even if there is a narrative driven by one figure more than the rest (for example, Jimmy Porter in *Look Back in Anger*), the story is, because of the absence of the novel-based narrative voice, enacted in a very different way. The device of dialogue actually contradicts the concept of the single central figure and therefore of many of the conventional notions of character, which are derived from the novel.

In all the approaches and methods offered in the how-to books the dominant recommended way of working leaves writing dialogue till last. For the rest, advice depends almost entirely on prose-based ways of translating thinking and imagining on to the page. Plans, outlines, scenarios, scene-by-scene breakdowns, while they are all analytically important, continually delay the moment when material out of which the work is actually made (dialogue) begins.

Not surprisingly, then, the assumption is made again and again that the way in to writing drama is through writing monologues. Or, to put it another way, that the way in to writing dialogue is through writing monologue. The argument also goes that because drama is 'based' on character, and/or because the dramatist has to construct the characters before the dialogue arrives, the 'voice' of the character in the monologue enables dialogue-based writing to be done better. This is not so. It conflates and confuses the processes of preparatory thinking, imagining and analysing (vital as these are at different points and in different ways) with the literary form itself. Drama is again usurped in a pedagogy which privileges the writing of prose, through the monologue.

Monologue and prose

At its most fundamental, monologue is a form of short story. When performed, it becomes dramatic storytelling, but it does not become drama just because it is performed. The proverbial idea that a brilliant performer can make even the telephone directory vivid is a tribute to the art of performance, not a statement that the telephone directory 'is' drama. The contemporary monologue developed after 1968 as an opportunistic form, either to provide material for auditions, or to incorporate storytelling forms as (a) ways to represent 'inner life' and (b) to include polemical elements, or messages.

Attitudes to monologues, or soliloquies, have varied across the centuries. At the turn of the twentieth century Archer announced that he did not favour asides and that soliloquies were out of fashion. This did not, however, lead him to any clear conclusions about dialogue: 'it does not seem very profitable to try to concentrate into a definition the distinctive qualities of dramatic dialogue.'[1] Baker optimistically remarked that the advent of naturalistic dialogue at the end of the nineteenth century (in parallel with the naturalistic novel) effectively dispensed with the soliloquy. Like Archer, he warned against resorting to monologue, because it described and replaced action which would be interrupted if another character

[1] Archer, op. cit., p. 225.

were onstage.[2] In other words like stage directions, it was a substitute for drama itself.

The monologue – in the form of a very long speech by a single character, generally given when there is no other character onstage – returned to dramatic writing during the 1960s and 1970s. Influenced in part by Brecht's use of direct address to the audience in the middle of scenes, and also perhaps by ideologies derived from the oral history movement, which privileged the individual voices of women, minorities and under-represented social groups, the monologue had an ideological, sociological and artistic place in drama. At the same time increased interest in the psychological and emotional make-up of characters (treating them *as if* they were real people) provided an aesthetic rationale. As Alan Ayckbourn has put it, 'Long speeches are good ways to reveal the inner thoughts and feelings of your characters.'[3]

However, during the 1970s monologues, or very long uninterrupted speeches, were also ways to convey historical or biographical information (research) in a quick narrative fashion. In sections of Caryl Churchill's plays, *Vinegar Tom* and *Light Shining in Buckinghamshire*, the first commissioned by Monstrous Regiment, the second by Joint Stock and both produced in 1976,[4] the politically conscious historical play, playing out the cross oppressions of class and gender, incorporated polemical elements in long speeches, which also conveyed what the 'character' 'felt'.

The monologue has remained in fashion in a more conventional storytelling form-within-a-play in the drama of Conor McPherson. For example, *The Weir*, first performed in 1997, has a number of long speeches and, effectively, monologues up to three pages long, in which the Irish tradition of oral storytelling is reproduced as part of the fabric of the play.[5] This works as both cultural tribute, and also as a way to move between storytelling prose and drama proper.

[2] Baker, op. cit., p. 392.
[3] Ayckbourn, op. cit., p. 71.
[4] *Plays: 1* by Caryl Churchill (Methuen, 1985).

Monologues are consistently present in all the how-to books as a kind of think-tank device, through which the student can develop her/his own ideas about the 'characters'. The fact that this is done through prose fiction gives the illusion that the drama is under way, while the exercise is, in fact, little more than note-taking. Pike and Dunn follow their discussion of character with a suggestion to write a monologue for each character.

Castagno suggests a range of different kinds of monologue, including one based on the recording of a sports commentator, to develop approaches to language register. He comments that interpolating a monologue between sections of dialogue can provide an effective strategy for discovering a character's function and thematic values without drafting scenes.[6] Precisely. It is selling the dramatic imagination short. Yeger recommends writing projects at the end of each chapter, suggesting that students observe a person and then write a monologue for them. All these are techniques for procrastination, for putting off the moment when the genre-specific work itself begins, and directing the imagination towards prose.

Even the best and most meticulous how-to drama-writing books by Noel Greig and Jean-Claude van Italie privilege monologue before dialogue. Greig, whose book is the most perceptive and detailed of all those currently available, grafts writing drama on to a general foundation of creative writing. The first part of his book habituates students to the process of observation and imaginative writing in ways which would be equally at home in more general CW texts. For example, he suggests writing a description of a room, using each of the five senses, and also writing a series of monologues for different people on the subject of love, to explore different kinds of speech patterns and attitudes. In themselves, of course, any kind of writing work or practice is always going to be useful. That is not the main issue.

What is important is that the first-person narrative voice entailed

---

[5] *The Weir* by Conor McPherson (Nick Hern Books, 1998).
[6] Castagno, op. cit., p. 141.

in monologue is not drama in the writing. It may be fun and productive, and stimulate the imagination, but it is also blocking access to the appropriate written form, which is to convey the matter only through dialogue, through individuated and interactive reactive speeches. To leave dialogue writing until last and then to give it short shrift is thus to deny the very centre of the drama-writing learning process. Eric Bentley commented, 'What sets dialogue off from the rest of literature is precisely dialogue, as opposed to monologue, verbal intercourse as opposed to verbal discourse.'[7] It is from this point that really learning the art of writing drama begins.

[7] *Life of the Drama*, p. 78.

10   The text – dialogue and relationships

So what exactly is dialogue? In a purely pragmatic way it can be compared to everyday conversation, to the verbal exchanges between people, which bind the way we live our social and personal lives. But in its literary form, as the *sine qua non* of dramatic writing, it is something rather different. It is not mere imitation of speech, even where it appears most realistic. As anyone knows who has listened carefully to spontaneous conversation, the latter is full of gaps and interruptions, of conscious and unconscious applications of register. Recording and transcribing any casual conversation illustrates this clearly. There is an additional complication, which is that – at one level – the test of the written product – the performance end – is subjected to the process of enunciation, in context. It is not conversation. It is dialogue. Dialogue can be naturalistic, poetic, elliptical, written in verse. It has its own literary and stylistic conventions.

I am aware that, like other books about writing drama, I am addressing dialogue rather late on. However, I am doing so for completely different reasons. It is not because it is the least important, or the easiest, or something which can only be done (relatively easily) after 'everything else' has been decided. It is precisely the opposite. It is because it is the *most* important (how could it be otherwise?), because it is the *only* significant (and signifying) literary means whereby the dramatic text can be imagined and written. Because this seems to be such a rare view in the literature, I have had to prepare the ground for discussing dialogue as the practice at the centre of the pedagogic approach. My advocacy of dialogue in a pedagogic context is different. I work almost entirely in and with dialogue in class, with students working exclusively with dialogue from the very beginning.

So what, exactly, is dialogue in the context of writing drama? 'The root word is the Greek *dialogos*, meaning conversation or discourse, and this has passed through Latin and French into English.'[1] Dialogue in prose fiction shares a particular temporal feature with the drama, but does so in quite a distinct way; and both deployments of dialogue are distinct from the ranges of everyday verbal discourse in which we all engage. The latter is often thought of as spontaneous, or relatively so, but it is also differently formalised and structured, on the basis of differently socially appropriate 'registers'. So, for example, the language one might use in a meeting with a bank manager will be determined by the context and purpose of the discussion, and also by the relative relationship of the participants: a discussion about a bank loan presupposes a variant on certain kinds of power relations. Dialogue between lovers will (not always, of course) carry the possibility of intimacy and the use of a language 'normally' only available in private. Conversations between a parent and child will be similarly determined – by age, the day-to-day functions of such exchanges and many other factors.

Dialogue, action and speech acts

In both the critical literature on drama and in the how-to books the notion of action (with conflict as a sequencing sub-category) is given prominence. Drama, it is said, 'must have' action; drama, it is implied or suggested, is built round the idea of action. In terms of

---

[1] Raymond Williams, *Writing in Society*, p. 31.

discussion about how the action is shaped, how it might or should be directed towards conflict, possible crisis and some kind of denouement, resolution or ending, it is clear that the concept of 'action' is to drama as the concept of 'narrative' is to the novel.

Confusingly, however, it also carries (explicitly or implicitly) the idea that 'action' in some way is likely to be, should be, or must be, physical rather than verbal. While this is entirely valid as one possibility, it privileges the physical over the emotional and verbal. A tension or contradiction is thus often set up between a rather crude notion of 'action' and the knowledge that (for example) emotional or psychological events or 'actions' also form part of the dramatic experience (action driving narrative) on both sides of the footlights and via the written text.

Even before semiology and performance theory addressed drama directly, there have been occasional perceptions that the concept of action can be extended to apply to dialogue. John Howard Lawson commented, 'Speech is a kind of action, *a compression and extension of action*. When a man speaks he performs an act . . .'[2] From a more contemporary theoretical point of view, Aston and Savona have pointed out that 'traditionally, action in drama has only been considered in terms of external action, but semioticians have tried to show how the use of language also constitutes a form of action'.[3]

One of the theoretical bridges between the study of everyday uses of language and formalised speech in drama is speech act theory. Philosopher J. L. Austin delivered a series of twelve William James lectures at Harvard in 1955, based on work he had begun at the end of the 1930s.[4] In Lecture 2 he commented that 'to *say* something is to *do* something . . . *by* saying or *in* saying something we are doing something'.[5] This is linked with a very specific idea of social 'performance': 'the idea of a performative utterance was that it was

---

[2] Lawson, op. cit., p. 288.
[3] Aston and Savona, op. cit., p. 55.
[4] *How to do Things with Words* by J. L. Austin (Harvard University Press, 1975).
[5] Ibid., p. 12.

to be (or to be included as part of) the performance of an action. Actions can only be performed by persons, and obviously in our cases the utterer must be the performer . . .'[6]

John R. Searle's book, subtitled 'An Essay in the Philosophy of Language', drew on work in cognitive science and linguistics, starting with a basic question: 'How do words relate to the world?'[7] 'Speaking a language is engaging in a (highly complex) rule-governed form of behaviour. To learn and master a language is (*inter alia*) to learn and to have mastered these rules.'[8] Since speaking a language is, effectively, performing 'speech acts', 'a theory of language is part of a theory of action, simply because speaking is a rule-governed form of behaviour'.[9]

From the point of view of understanding some of the complexities of what happens when people speak, Searle suggested 'there are a series of analytic connections between the notion of speech acts, what the speaker means, what the sentence (or any other linguistic element) uttered means, what the speaker intends, what the hearer understands, and what the rules governing the linguistic elements are.'[10] In the context of drama, this can be taken to refer to and cover concepts that are expressed through terms such as subtext and motivation. Clearly, underneath each line which is spoken is a whole edifice of what is *not* spoken. The concept of motivation thus returns us to the notion of character in a way which, in its turn, diverts away again from dialogue itself.

These brief references to speech act theory enable us to see how it prioritises dialogue in drama in an illuminating way virtually ignored by most other how-to books. If speech (dialogue) is understood as one of the forms of action, and if action is held to be at the core of drama, then the art of writing dialogue must be given

---

[6] Ibid., p. 60.
[7] *Speech Acts* by John R. Searle (Cambridge University Press, 1969), p. 3.
[8] Ibid., p. 12.
[9] Ibid., p. 17.
[10] Ibid., p. 21.

its rightful prominence. The assumption that it will simply some-how follow on planning and character summaries assumes that all work on dialogue is external to its practice-based procedures in writing.

However, even speech act theory is not entirely appropriate for dialogue. In its valuable attention to the nature and variety and categorisation of individual utterances, and of their utterance by individuals, it bears some similarity with the post-novelistic foregrounding of 'character' as the motor and motivator of dramatic action. Again, we are steered away from dialogue itself.

Dialogue and voicing

The individuation of some aspects of linguistic speech theory, along with the stress on individual character, and characterisation, conceals the complex nature and interactive social function of both speech and of dialogue. A differently angled approach, which allows for both social as well as language-based perspectives, has come from the renewed interest in Bakhtin, referred to in chapter 5. However, in the context of writing drama this becomes more complex.

Raymond Williams has pointed out: 'It is impossible to read "dramatic writing" adequately unless we are aware that it is writing for speech in many voices and for action.'[11] He linked this not just to drama from the past, but to a significant literary form, which was revived during the Italian Renaissance: 'There is a familiar kind of written argument in which the method is the representation of different positions, and of exchanges between them, through the arranged alternating speech of named persons or elements. This has been common in philosophy and related arguments since Plato . . .'[12] Williams's reference to 'multivocal speech' reminds us that 'it is

[11] *Writing in Society*, pp. 4–5.
[12] Ibid., p. 31.

almost universally assumed . . . that dramatic dialogue is a representation of people speaking to each other, in the simplest sense'.[13]

This shifting between speech in everyday life and its contexts, and speech as represented in writing, on the page (dialogue), which then is transformed into an encoded, artificial, fictionalised enunciation in performance, shows how complex the exchange between spoken and written language is. Referring to Derrida's distinction between written and spoken language, Elinor Fuchs has pointed 'to the particular premise that dramatic performance traditionally imitates the hierarchy of speech/writing that Derrida locates in the Western philosophical tradition as a whole. That is, drama has evolved as the form of writing that strives to create the illusion that it is composed of spontaneous speech . . .'[14]

When it is on the page, written dialogue may or may not resemble spontaneous speech, depending on the style in which it is composed; however, in performance, which privileges the immediacy, the nowness, the present-momentness of dialogue, no matter what the style of the writing, the appearance of spontaneity must, at all times, be the quality to which the enunciation and effect aspires and which rehearsal attains. However much performers and audience may know that weeks of preparation have preceded the performance, each individual presentation is 'as if' happening for the very first time at that moment, in complete spontaneity.

Dialogue – turn-taking, exchange

Raymond Williams has pointed out that 'The idea of dialogue, even in its variable forms, presumes a form of exchange. This is represented in modern information theory in A-B or A-B-C models

[13] Ibid., p. 32.
[14] Fuchs, op. cit., p. 74.

and diagrams, with arrows of interaction.'[15] Aston and Savona, advocating 'a systematic approach to dialogue analysis', have characterised dialogue as being 'structured as a turn-taking system'.[16] Castagno describes this further: 'Turns relate dialogue to pairs of speakers.'[17]

Eric Bentley has encapsulated the fundamental contradiction within dramatic dialogue: 'it is the first person that is dominant. Dramatic discourse is egocentric: the speaking subject defines everything (including the you-addressee) in terms of his [sic] own place in the dramatic world.'[18] In further amplification: 'The speech event is, in its own right, the chief form of interaction in the drama. The dialogic exchange, that is, does not merely . . . *refer* deictically to the dramatic action but directly *constitutes* it . . . carried, above all, by the intersubjective force of discourse.'[19]

In the context of dramatic dialogue, the speech event is, of course, the individual 'utterance' of each 'character' at any given moment. That is why the idea that each character must have her/his own idiosyncratic 'voice' – i.e., dialect, speech patterns, rhythms etc. – is appropriate, no matter what the style of writing (on the whole). However, a play is not made up of a series of isolated speech acts, any more than everyday conversation is. Nor is it merely a matter of 'taking turns', although speakers do, in drama, tend to alternate, rather than overlap or interrupt each other, while still able to carry on their interaction. It is not even a matter of exchange. Alternation is the procedure whereby the speakers relate to each other and, as Bentley wrote, 'constitute' the action.

The dependence of dramatic dialogue on what is called 'deixis' has been noted by more than one writer. Deixis refers to those tiny words which refer to place or person, from within the action, as it

---

[15] Williams, op. cit., p. 60.
[16] Aston and Savona, op. cit., p. 52.
[17] Castagno, op. cit., p. 100.
[18] *The Theory of the Modern Stage* by Eric Bentley (Penguin, 1968), p. 143.
[19] Ibid., pp. 156–7.

were: 'here', 'there'; or to time: 'now', 'after'; to objects: 'this', 'that'; or to another person, without naming her/him: 'you', 'he'. In the context of both conversation and dramatic dialogue, these short-hand elements or (in the theory of socio-linguist Basil Bernstein) uses of 'restricted code' make complete sense to the participants. Two friends in the same room can refer to objects around them, to each other and to other people they know; they can use the word 'this' to refer to a table, without having to use the word 'table'. They are inside the situation, and are responsible for creating and perpetuating it together.

Reaction and interaction: dialogue and relationships

As characters talk, speak, exchange speech acts, however, there is another crucial element, which extends beyond the idea of exchange and interaction: that is, that every single speech, line, phrase, word, is also, and at every point, *reaction* or *response* to both the sum and the detail of everything which has gone before. Considering this from the other side of the footlights, as it were, from the point of view of the performer, this is automatically understood throughout the process of rehearsal and performance. Cicely Berry, voice, text and dialogue coach, has written of 'how each character is changed by what another character has spoken, and how their very choice of words affects how he/she replies'.[20] Examples of exercises she uses with performers include asking each performer to repeat the last word spoken to him/her or a phrase from that speech, before he/she replies with his/her own line, to highlight the way in which each speech provokes the next.

Dialogue, building from the very first line, becomes a complex edifice, a highly structured verbal creation in which no line or

[20] Berry, op. cit., p. 140.

speech can be considered or understood except in relation to a series of reactive eddies outwards into the rest of the drama. No wonder it is so difficult to understand and define, and no wonder (in a sense) that there is a desire to resort to what looks simple and graspable: the idea of the individual voice and individual character (the human agents who carry the action/narrative). Students need, above all, to be able to move from the more common and familiar ability to write single-voiced narrative into writing multi-voiced dialogue.

Response as the condition of dialogue

Dramatic dialogue is, and constructs, relationships in reactive, interdependent interaction, in a constant state of responsiveness. 'Response' is the only inevitable condition of dialogue. Writing dramatic dialogue, therefore, consists of imagining and writing *relationships*, not speeches and not individual speech acts. The 'action' – emotional, psychological – is what happens 'between' speeches and the moment-by-moment study each performer gives to his/her part consists of a series of decisions about what is happening *between* speeches, in order to establish what and how each speech is uttered. There is a temporal accumulation of dialogue: as the narrative/drama progresses, the edifice becomes more and more complex.

Relationships and character

The individuated concept of character, which reaches back to Aristotelian notions of a central 'hero', which in its turn finds echo in the individuated narrative voices of the novel, jostles up against the concept of relationships in the drama. If there were only ever two 'characters' in a drama, this might be a relatively simple matter of just *one* relationship being written/explored. But, to compound matters, the more characters in the drama, the more breathtakingly compounded is the number of relationships to be imagined and written by the dramatist.

Two figures constitute one relationship (from two points of view).

Figure 1

Three figures constitute seven relationships in all:

Figure 2

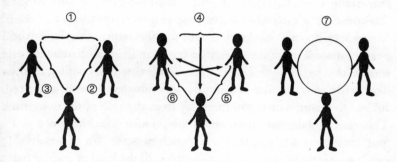

Four figures constitute a total of twenty-five relationships, in different numerical permutations and combinations. Draw the figures and do the sums! Five figures, in different combinations and permutations, add up to 121 relationships. If four or five characters are onstage at once, then the number of relationships the dramatist is carrying in his/her head (consciously or not) is breathtaking. This helps to demonstrate why some people find it hard to imagine in dramatic terms and to write drama. In prose they can inhabit the singular dramatic narrative voice, and in poetry (especially lyric poetry) the leading 'voice' is also more likely to be singular.

In class I demonstrate this on the floor. Two students face each other. The space between them shows clearly that this is one relationship. Add a third, stand them in a triangle again facing each other, and this tests the rest of the class to count up the number of relationships. Four students test this even more, and so on. Now the secret is out!

To add to all the reasons given so far, this is another overwhelming reason for writing dialogue from the start. It is challenging enough to carry a narrative in a relationship between two voices (human agents/characters), in which each can only articulate in the dramatic first person. To do so with more relationships, building and alternating, is even more complex. It takes practice and training to be able to do so in such a way that everything – narrative, relationships, individuation – is carried via this constant twining and intertwining play of relationships.

Experiments in writing monologue simply confirm this. However neatly turned a monologue may be for an individual 'character', as soon as that figure comes into interaction (existential conflict, if you like) with another, the apparently individuated speech acts are subject to manipulation and interplay from the other human agent. This conceptualisation lies behind the popular idea that once you 'put' characters onstage, they will somehow 'speak for themselves', or 'take over the action'. They do nothing of the kind of course; but they *are* subject to the responsive controls of the dialogue (other human agents) as well as the narrative in which they are placed.

11 Teaching and learning the art of writing drama

As all teachers and students know, the quicksilver ambience and activity of the classroom is virtually impossible to document accurately. Teachers sometimes describe the way they work, aiming to create an impression of the atmosphere, as well as a blow-by-blow account of the pedagogic process that happens. Creative writing texts cannot, by definition, re-create the workshop in which students bring in pieces of writing for the class to discuss. They consist, therefore, mostly of writing 'exercises', as ways to encourage students and readers to generate and develop their writing. But however stimulating these may sometimes be, no exercise can ever fully substitute for the living exchange in the classroom. And such a procedure is constantly piecemeal, dealing with new pieces of writing, rather than building cumulatively week by week.

My approach to teaching is very different. I did not set out to be different just for the sake of it. Like most other writers who teach imaginative writing, I made it up as I went along. I developed ways of teaching which sharpened my own understanding of the way I write drama, and, gradually evolved a structured way of teaching writing in class. Each week tested the developmental and cumulative nature of the learning process. As I read literature about creative writing and met other teachers, I became aware that I was developing rather differently inflected sets of pedagogic priorities from those enshrined in the literature and other approaches to teaching.

CW literature argues that creative writing workshops depart from conventional academic assumptions. For example, creative writing is presented as a 'practice-based' form of teaching and learning – acquiring knowledge and understanding by 'doing'. By analogy with other art forms – music, drama, dance, the visual arts – imaginative writing clearly must be developed and practised. However, in a structured educational context there is, I believe, also an obligation to push the boundaries further; to think about, to study and to expand student understanding of the cultural context in which their particular genre is located, with due attention given to analytic and intellectually searching work. This must mean studying the history of drama on the page and in performance, and exploring dramatic criticism and literary theory.

Aims and boundaries

First of all, it must be absolutely clear that the pedagogy of the art of writing drama is neither a training for professional dramatists, nor a proto-therapeutic exercise in self-expression. It is, of course, entirely possible that undergraduate and/or postgraduate students may indeed go on to write for the dramatic professions and each student may gain emotional satisfaction from the process, but the discipline is no different from any other educational experience. English students may go on to write important critical or theoretical books; or not. History students may go on to do original research and write about it; or not. Music students may end up as performers; or not. Graduates and non-graduates in all kinds of subjects may end up writing drama. A training in writing drama is not, and cannot be, determined by the imperatives of an employment-based outcome. This does not gainsay enthusiasm or ambition. The point about educational training is that it provides an opportunity to study, explore, deconstruct, think about, as well as practise the art form.

The base-line aim for a course in the art of writing drama is that each student should, ultimately, develop an increased understanding of the relationship between her/his own imagination and the various dramatic conventions which determine the translation and transformation of that imagination onto the page, making it available for transformation onto the stage. This entails:

1. Imaginative acuity, involving each student's ability to deploy, or begin to deploy, his/her own individual resources: cultural, linguistic, imaginative and intellectual. This is developed via an incremental understanding of how to think about, discover and explore different kinds of subject matter, incorporating active research and knowledge seeking and then to transform these into dialogue.
2. Textual acuity: verbal, and aural, developed and refined through writing, analysing and hearing dialogue, and through the movement from page to stage and back again.
3. Spatial acuity: through an ongoing and active movement from page to stage (classroom space) and back again.
4. Temporal acuity: through an understanding of the relationship between different timescales: within the imaginative work and in staged-completed performance running time. A real understanding of presentness, and the immediacy of performance and the way this is refracted in writing dialogue; the drama's past and its treatment of time.
5. Analytical acuity: the ability to hear both the literal moment of the dialogue and to analyse the possibilities for development inherent in it.
6. Acuity of convention: in the same way that it is necessary to understand the historical and contemporary conventions of prose fiction and poetry, to study and explore the resources and conventions (historical and contemporary) of dramatic writing. In an ideal pedagogic set-up, this would involve some prior writing-based study of prose fiction and poetry.

Through class work, students need to acquire a practical and analytical understanding of the following:

1. The way narrative in drama is constructed through dialogue in interactive relationships of varying complexity.
2. Ways in which drama is structured through scenes, 'beats' and 'units', if such terminology is useful, and how each scene relates to the balance of the whole piece. Each scene always contains a pivotal point or moment, around which the narrative is structured. This must be understood through careful analysis. Understanding of different inflections of cause-and-effect in narrative.
3. A developed grasp of differently voiced and inflected dialogue, achieved through an understanding of register, and the ways in which register and different speech-defined forms of articulation interact.
4. The importance of completing short plays within the classroom time and course length. The text is absolutely as complete as it can be, because that is what the dramatist does. The dramatist *must* imagine, conceive, write, rewrite, structure, refine, begin, middle and end, within the conventions and devices available to the dramatic writing process.
5. Use of scenarios or plans only as relevant, at different directed moments of the writing process and never at the beginning.
6. Complete freedom with regard to subject matter. Notions of 'idea', 'premise', discussions of subject matter and theme are highly significant, but to be explored post hoc, or, if relevant, along the way, not foreclosed at the start.

Such an achieved set of awarenesses, through the production and discussion of dramatic fiction in the classroom, does not amount to a training for professional dramatists. After all, the drama has and will sustain itself perfectly well without any formal training in the art of writing drama. The great advantage of the fact that drama writing has moved into the academy is that opportunities can be provided for study, understanding and practice for a range of people who might otherwise remain outside the benefits of such exploratory time.

12 The pedagogic process

This chapter is as accurate an account as I can give about the way I teach. This is not just a narcissistic indulgence. It is my attempt to convey the ways in which I implement the principles and theorising which comprise the rest of this book. My teaching approach did not develop 'out of' or 'from' theory. The theorising evolved as my approach evolved and as I became clearer in my thinking, so my teaching in turn also modified. Writing this book has been a way of rounding up, making coherent and codifying the combination of theory and practice, which I believe can help transform the art of writing drama. This is a practical, as well as a polemical, aim. I deploy this approach in both adult education and in university courses. Reading lists, where I compile and require them, are modified according to the educational context.

All my work, and all the learning, is based on writing done by students in class. Over the course of each term, or module, each student produces a complete short play, written in class, cumulatively built up and explored at every stage, on the page and in the classroom space. At no stage are value judgements used during the exploration or analysis of scenes. In formal courses assignments are produced at the end, written independently by each student outside the classroom and these are marked in the usual way. In this respect, teaching the art of writing drama is no different from any other academic subject. Teacher–student contact provides the information and builds the expertise, and assignments are evidence of the student's ability to translate his/her understanding into independent work.

Overheard conversations

Aural and verbal acuity is developed in a number of different ways. Ongoing weekly 'homework' is particularly important in this process. This consists of requiring students to write down any overheard conversation (or fragment of a conversation) between two people verbatim during the week. These can come from *any* conversation, anywhere and about anything. Bring in at least one, I say. Carry around a notebook, so that if you are somewhere and remember, you can write stuff down. Do not judge or make any kind of decision about whether it is an 'interesting' or 'important' conversation. No value judgements. The only important thing is to remember to do it, have paper and pen, and get it written down on the spot, exactly as you are hearing it.

At the beginning of each class we go round and hear these snippets, without explanation or discussion. Even a relatively simple-seeming task such as this reveals some interesting issues. Many students apologise because what they have written isn't 'interesting'. This can go on for weeks. Suspending judgement is not always easy for people. Sometimes it is just an excuse not to do the exercise, even though I explain very carefully, repeatedly, that it is a very important part of the process. It tests the circle between ear, mind and the act of listening, hearing, retaining, writing, refining memory and practice. It is similar to what happens if someone has to take notes during a lecture; the difference is that my requirement is that the words they hear and the words on the page must be the same, verbatim. If someone hears a conversation but is unable to write it down on the spot, the exercise is still worth doing at home although it then becomes an unverifiable test of memory.

Some people will just turn up with one line. This is fine as a first stab, but I suggest that, even if they just bring two lines from two different speakers, they should concentrate on the moment of exchange. This directs attention not only to the words themselves, but to the moment of initiation, of reaction, embedded in dialogue. This can take students some time, since their attention must be divided between two voices. It helps to transfer the concept of imaginative writing from prose-related practices to dialogue-related procedures.

Alternatively, students may turn up with a page and a half of dialogue and will claim that yes, they did hear it all and yes, they did write it down exactly as they heard it at the time. Given that we write more slowly than we speak, this is clearly a case of great economy with the truth. Such students basically want to show off and will have made up some, if not all, of the dialogue. I stress that the exercise is not about finding ways to begin a scene and then continue it (in other circumstances this might be interesting).

Sometimes students will precede the reading by starting off on long anecdotal explanations of where they were and what was going on. I interrupt and say that all that is irrelevant; all that is important is the dialogue, which we hear just as it is. This is a preparation and reminder of the relative 'bareness' of dialogue on the air and to encourage our focus as listeners not just on individual speakers, but on what happens at the moment of exchange and interaction, between speeches.

When I ask students to read out the overheard conversations, I preface the first session by saying you can either read it yourself together with someone else, or give it to two other people to read. There will always be at least one student who wants to read the whole thing him- or herself: no one will be able to read my handwriting, they say. Fine, I say. Go ahead. The student begins to read and after a few lines, I stop him/her. What are we hearing? I ask. Various answers are given. The significant issue is that if one person reads out dialogue spoken by two people, what we are actually hearing is a single voice and (effectively) a monologue. This is obvious, once it is articulated or written down, but it is never obvious to students unused to the difference between written and spoken dialogue. It often takes time, and sometimes a long time, for students to internalise the difference between the excitement of a singular mind (the student) imagining and writing in more than one literary 'voice' on the page, and its translation into multiple voices. Everyone can write dialogue without thinking about it, but it takes time to understand what it is and to develop the skills to think about it.

Occasionally the ethics of the process will come up; sometimes people understandably feel self-conscious about writing down the conversation of strangers. Some will think it an intrusive thing to do. This can lead to a very interesting discussion about the way we feel/think about the ownership of our words and what happens if someone else appropriates them. By extension, it can lead at a later date to discussions about 'using' real life experiences, which might involve other people, as part of the source material for fiction.

Languages and individual resources

Early in the first class I go round the class and ask everyone about the language(s) they speak. I am careful only to ask about language and occasionally, just to clarify, if a student is bilingual, I might ask about where he/she grew up or went to school and learned language. The 'personal' questions go no further. During the process there is usually at least one person who says he/she speaks 'ordinary' or 'standard' English. This generates some discussion about the kind of English students thinks they speak, whether there might be some kind of regional or dialect-based element in the background – indeed, about how many 'Englishes' we all acquire and use during the course of our lives. At a later stage this might lead to a more formal discussion of register and the ways in which language is differently inflected, depending on different situations and relationships, and how each individual produces such languages as part of her/his own 'idiolect'. Without this kind of understanding to underpin it, discussion about the right 'tone' for each character is likely to be vague and idiosyncratic.

Out of this discussion, at the beginning, and again later if it is relevant and productive, I actively encourage people to write in their other/first language(s) as well as in their various Englishes. Sometimes students might mix two languages, or even write whole scenes in another language. If I ask them to translate, so that we have two versions of the scene, the purpose is not merely for the rest of us to understand, but primarily for these students to explore how 'their' own languages interrelate and how they can be used as an imaginative and cultural resource. Matters of rhythm, pace, stress, the structure of sentences, idioms and a whole host of other linguistic elements resonate with possibilities for each student. Language is both shared and individuated. Importantly, again and again I have been delighted to see that exploring these different languages can lead to different cultural and social subject matter without explicitly raising this as a possibility. The way in through language enables each student (if she/he wants to) to explore her/his own distinctive imaginative resources and find material which interests her/him. More often than not, writing in another language leads to heightened, surer and more subtle applications of English(es).

When a student writes in another language, other members of the class are likely to find themselves reading a scene aloud in French, or Italian, or even a non-European language. It doesn't matter whether they can understand the words or not. It is extraordinary how a student who clearly will never make a performer (this is not an acting class, so it doesn't matter), when she/he is reading a scene in Italian, will suddenly change her/his body language and gestures without even being aware of it. A whole different take on dialogue and subject matter is opened up. Through language, important areas of cultural experience and subject matter come into the writing, all within the student's choice and control.

Words on the page, in the air and on the floor

Each three-hour class is structured in more or less the same way. After the overheard conversations are read out each week, without comment or discussion, but always to a great deal of pleasure and entertainment, there is either a writing session of between ten and twenty minutes, or the completion of a round of work read aloud from the previous week.

In the very first class the writing session begins after some brief opening discussion about language. All writing sessions are accompanied by a small number of 'rules', which are not initially explained, but which are later explored on the floor. The rules are quite simple: 1, no stage directions and 2, no monologues. Depending on what kind of scenes people write, later there may be some supplementary rules (though these always come with explanations): no telephone calls, no flashbacks, no therapists. No speech to run for more than three or four lines on the page.

Surrounding all these is the primacy of the most difficult element for students to grasp: the immediacy, the present moment of the dialogue, the relationships and the first-person inhabitation of each speaking voice/persona. I tend not to use the word 'character' until much later in the process, if at all. For the sake of a kind of simplicity, and in order to sidestep whatever expectations students come with, I usually refer to the 'people' or 'figures' or 'voices' in the scene.

The first 'instruction', then, is to write a particular kind of scene, with just two people in it. I am deliberately not spelling out the kind of scene I suggest, because each teacher needs to be free to evolve whatever starting point will yield material with which he/she can work.

From a classroom in which there has been an informal conversational mode of exchange, we move into a moment in which the room is filled with small pieces of art, all built just out of dialogue. Initially students are not aware of this change, but gradually the experience becomes more familiar as the weeks pass. If someone is unsure how to start writing, I suggest an opening line. Work thus begins immediately with dialogue. There is never any need to explain what dialogue is, although sometimes I need to explain briefly how to set out the dialogue on the page. My experience has been that most people who come to these classes will never have seen a published play, or read any drama on the page.

Next, all the scenes are read, one after the other (with each 'character' separately voiced) with no comment or discussion. The next stage is to go round the room again, to hear each scene read again, stopping briefly after each scene to begin the structural and analytic process. This generates a pattern of analysis, which is repeated, with cumulatively different issues explored each time. After this first piece of writing I choose one of a number of basic very open questions. So it might be whether it is clear, from the dialogue alone, what the genders of the voices are. It doesn't matter what the student who has written it thinks; we judge *only* from aural evidence in the text. Or the question might be what relationship the two voices might have with each other. Again, evidence *must* come from within the text, direct or circumstantial evidence.

The second piece of homework is that each week students are asked to type up their scenes, making as many copies as there are voices, without extending the scenes, or rewriting them. From the second week on there will be two copies of each scene and if the number of characters expands, to a maximum of five for such a short play, there will be the appropriate number of copies made. If a student has not made copies the scene cannot be read out, since each performer needs his/her own copy. Again, while this sounds obvious, if not trite, experiencing it in practice reveals how centred we all are on the individually voiced text.

Scenes on the air and behind the fourth wall

In the first week students read from their seats in a large circle, radiating out from my desk. Facing me at the top of the classroom is a gap with no chairs. This, effectively, makes the room into an informal theatre, with a huge space in the middle. A couple of chairs function as rudimentary indicators of set. From the second week everyone's scene (or scenes, as they accumulate) are read out again on the floor. Each student casts his/her own scene(s) and they have the option of either being in their own scenes or watching others read them. Generally, however, they prefer to watch. I comment that it is important that everyone must get an opportunity to perform, so that each student knows what happens, what is involved and what it is like to be on the other side of the dramatic text; in other words to move across the fourth wall into the performance text. This is neither as obvious nor as easy as it might sound, even in an adult education class, where some of the students may already have acting experience. I have a strict routine for how this is set up, to give students some idea of the degree of precision and discipline involved in even the simplest form of performance.

My instructions, from the second week on, are always the same; I have found they need to be repeated each week. The transformation from seated person-student into the completely imagined person, in relationship with others who are making the same transformation (i.e., performer/character), produces some taxing experiences and processes. In addition, every time a scene is enacted the space itself is transformed.

If someone has forgotten to make a copy I delay the reading of their scene. It's all right, they say, there are only two characters, we can share. I explain. If you are both sharing the same script, first of all it restricts the amount you can move around, because only one of you will be holding the script. This means that you both share a primary relationship to a piece of paper, rather than to each other, to the person to whom you are talking. With the right number of copies there are other instructions to be observed, each of which leads to a greater understanding of the nature of performance and the role of the performer and/or director.

First, make as much eye contact with the person to whom you are talking as possible. This entails compounding the relationship between the written, the spoken and the heard. It involves finding places to look up from the reading without interrupting the flow. It involves listening to the person who is talking to you, while preparing to respond with your own lines. In practice, this involves the eye taking in the next few words, which are still being spoken as the person returns her/his eye to the page, having also retained a visual memory of where she/he was. The acts of looking to and from the script are, in their microcosmic way, a means of constantly being reminded of the relationship between, and process of trans-formation from, written and performed text. This takes many people time to develop, but they all improve and therefore also sharpen their verbal, aural and visual acuity.

There must be no eye contact or conversation with anyone else sitting in the classroom. The audience, I say, does not exist. You do not know we are here. Students may have trouble with a word on the page and their instinct is to look at the student/author for clarification. Some may lose their place on the page and say 'sorry', or 'where was I', or 'whoops'. As soon as this happens (and it always does at some point) I stop the reading immediately and say we must go from the top, from the beginning of the scene.

I explain, of course. As soon as you speak, I say, you are doing a number of things: you are ad-libbing because you are speaking words that are not part of the text (no crime against that, but it is a skill in itself, relevant in a different kind of situation); you are jumping out of 'character' and speaking from your 'real' self and on the other side of the footlights your real self does not, and cannot, exist. Finally, you are ignoring or blurring or pretending that, or behaving as if, the fourth wall between performers and audience does not exist. This happens also when the performers giggle or whisper to each other in the middle of a scene. In your performer persona, all you have are the words on the page. There is nothing else.

The empty space against the wall facing me is the 'backstage' area. As soon as everyone has a copy of their script, I call them up to the backstage area. This often takes some time, since the first thing everyone does is bury their head in the words, to see what they are about to speak. This is symbolic of the entirely appropriate fact that they are each responsible for their own part, but it is also problematic, because it means they have not yet made the conceptual leap to an understanding that the fourth wall divides performers and audience, and that once they have gone to the performing end of the classroom they have become part of an entirely imaginary world and can/are about to relate only to each other.

If you exit from your scene, I say, do not come back and sit in the audience. We do not exist. We are not here. Your space remains in the imaginary world where, even when you are 'offstage', you are still part of the imaginary world. This takes a while for some people to absorb and understand. I repeat it. In some circumstances I might refer to Stanislavsky's idea of the 'circle of attention', but only if it helps to speed up the process. Most people who come to any kind of drama-writing class are not necessarily even familiar with his name and virtually no one has ever read any theory, or if they occasionally have, everything goes out of the window as they grapple with the work of writing and the practical implications of performance.

Each student thus constantly moves between writing and performance, so he/she can experience (hear, see and feel) the difference and the interaction. Acting ability is entirely irrelevant. It is not an acting class, though the presence of even one person who has done some acting can be exciting for everyone. The only thing I ask is that everything they say should be audible on the other side of the room. Everyone always participates. Everyone always becomes more comfortable in the space during the course, more expansive with their body language, very often prepared to do slightly unusual things, such as lying down, or hiding behind a chair. Everyone improves as a performer through the course.

If at any point you are unsure, I say, work it out in silence. It doesn't matter if the scene gets into a muddle. Silence and moving around do not break the atmosphere in the way that words do. This, in its own specific way, serves also to highlight the determining role in drama of the words, the dialogue.

Analysis and possibility

Each student's short play is built scene by scene, week by week. Each scene is analysed in terms of a series of very specific issues, out of which the possibilities for development emerge, each choice hopefully enhanced by greater understanding. This seems to be a relatively unusual way of working – the only other author of a how-to-write-drama book who seems to share some of this approach is Noel Greig. Even though, as I have pointed out, he also advocates leaving the dialogue to last, he comments, 'even the most basic text contains within it the potential seeds for further development. When working with writers on their plays, I have found that the best way of moving forward is to address the clues that the text already provides.'[1] Although he is referring to dramaturgical work done on already written plays, the same principle carefully developed and applied is, I am convinced, by far the best and most grounded way for each student to develop his/her writing in class.

If discussion of the first scene centres on questions about the relationship between the two people, the discussion proceeds without the participation of the student who has written the scene. Other students suggest different kinds of relationship, always, at my insistence, with verbal evidence from within the scene. If there is no obvious evidence (i.e., gender indicated by the names on the left, a

[1] Greig, op. cit., p. 31.

son calling his mother 'Mum', or just characters called A and B), then other students draw on related circumstantial evidence in the scene. Sometimes the scene might be read again, with the process helping to sharpen hearing, perception and memory of the writing. I always take notes and I regularly suggest to students that they too should take notes.

Such discussion often reveals social and cultural expectations. If a student suggests that a domestic scene might be a husband and wife, because the woman is serving dinner, if there is no actual evidence from within the scene, discussion might ensue about the possibility that it might be the man who is serving dinner. Discussions of possible relationships often become discussions about gender attribution and cultural expectation. Students may or may not have made their own decisions in writing their scenes, but even where gender is clearly indicated, rereading the scene with gender roles reversed can reveal all kinds of other relationships and storyline possibilities. Stereotypes may be observed, or they may be subverted. Students decide for themselves. The issue is never whether the class guesses 'right' or 'wrong', but rather what possibilities are revealed as already inherently there within the text. The student/writer's intentions are irrelevant to the discussion itself, and ultimately she/he always makes her/his own decisions. The analysis will always sharpen everyone's perception of the written and spoken text.

In anticipation of the next scene to be written, the first scene is read again and, still with close attention to the text and always quoting evidence from within the text, students are asked to think about what event might have preceded the one they have just heard and/or what event might follow it. This is a discussion of narrative, sequence and order, although not always explicitly identified as such at this stage. Again, we discuss only with evidence, what event might (at whatever distance of time) have preceded the one we have heard. There may be one obvious possibility, or there may be a number. For the next writing session each student decides whether he/she writes a scene that comes before, or a scene that comes after. I suggest that the time gap between scenes should be quite short – perhaps within the same day or the next.

Plan, event, conflict and subtext

When each student has written three scenes and we have explored a variety of issues in each scene, there is a planning session, dove-tailing in the scenes already written. Students are asked to write a plan for a short play, of between five and seven scenes (an odd number so that one scene can be at the centre). The scenes already written can be placed anywhere in this sequence. Each scene must be summarised in no more than two or three lines maximum, which describe the main event in the scene. No dialogue, I say; this is just a brief description of what happens.

People have many different ideas about what constitutes an 'event', or something that happens. It is only sometimes physical; more often than not it is something emotional. 'Susan feels betrayed by John.' Of course, this is an emotional event and entirely valid; but it only becomes dramatic if it is built round a narrative event.

This is a genuinely difficult matter. Words are 'acts' of a kind; a character feeling something strongly is also an event. The inter-active event is, in most cases, the key. Scene 1: A wants B to make a birthday cake for C. This is more than just the single 'want' of A (i.e., the conventional idea that a scene is driven by a character who 'wants' something). A character who wants something can want it till the cows come home, but it is only when there is someone else there, with something interactive happening, that there is an event. The idea of 'conflict' is often used as a way of expressing the inevitability of interaction, but it is misleading. Not that 'conflict', or opposition between two people is wrong or bad, but because the immanence of action/event in any exchange between two people makes the whole issue both simpler and more complex. In the end the definition of an action or event becomes contingent on the overall structure and on the ways in which events link together, lead to one another, or provoke each other.

A Will you make a cake?
B Yes.

Even this apparently simple exchange, which appears to conclude in agreement, contains contradictory possibilities. Yes (if you will help me). Yes (I would love to). Yes (I am lying). Yes (when it suits me). Exchange in and of itself is nuanced, from two different points of view, becoming communication across the gap of difference, even difference in similarity. This is an example of what dramatists can mean when they sometimes say that the real action is in the gaps between the dialogue. It is also what is encapsulated by the term 'subtext'. It is never a matter of 'putting' subtext in. There is always subtext, because there is always exchange and there is always an 'in-between'.

In the end it comes down to the way the drama is told or unfolds – the way the events or the happenings are linked together, rather than any abstract idea of what makes a 'good' story. We need only compare the murders and military events in Shakespeare's tragedies and history plays with the subtleties of emotional nuance in Samuel Beckett's *Waiting for Godot* to see how wide-ranging the concept of action, conflict and narrative are. This is partly historical, partly stylistic, partly based on cultural expectation.

What matters here is the way in which the student imagines or thinks the causal connections. After the plans are read out loud, we again go round, to spell out the cause-and-effect relationship between the one-line summary of scenes. The assumption must be that scene B happens because of scene A and that, without scene A, scene B could not take place. This logic can also be spelled out from the last scene backwards. During the rest of the course students write the remaining scenes, in any order they want, following the plan. If new events arise and different scenes become relevant, the plan is not cast in stone.

Time and place

With each plan, each scene summarising (with a bit of luck and nudging) a single pivotal event, we can discuss chronology, or time lines, or timescale. This too is always flexible. A short play – fifteen to twenty minutes, which is a manageable length within the time span of a term/semester – concentrates the mind. If someone wants to cover a hundred years in such a short time, while, in principle, anything is possible, in practice the idea enables us to discuss, from the point of view of time, how the narrative connections, the cause-and-effect patterns, might work over time. Causality and time are always in some kind of significant relationship. I ask each student to plot out a provisional timescale in his/her plan, and to decide on a notional overall timescale, so that the story/narrative is contained in time. I suggest keeping the time sensibly contained – a few months at most.

Some how-to books assert that a play's 'location' is crucially important. This is linked to the idea that everything must be decided before dialogue can be written. In practice, the matter of location (where scenes take place imaginatively, as well as how they take place within the performance space) has more fluidity than might at first appear. In the end, there is always an active relationship between location, what takes place and how it takes place.

Two lovers ending a relationship in a restaurant may do so differently if the same scene were set in private, in their shared kitchen. Here the differences are of contrast: an intimate, perhaps emotionally charged, encounter, which takes place in public, will have a built-in imaginary audience. In the privacy of a domestic setting emotional holds may not be barred. But it could work in precisely the opposite way. The private location could contrast with a clipped, indirect, restrained emotional encounter, while the public location might provoke an emotional explosion. In the end *what* happens in a scene is most important and that is determined by the narrative context. It does not need a stage direction to place it. The place can, very often indeed, be decided later.

The matter of location is something I explore on the floor, at appropriate moments during the course and generally at a later stage. While there are times when the location is glaringly obvious, most of the time there will be flexibility about where a scene or piece of dialogue may be set. A good example about the variability of location is often provided by television dramas. The American hospital series, *ER*, has numerous examples of a continuously written scene between two important characters, where the whole 'scene' is split up into different locations, which themselves provide an underlying narrative and sense of urgency in the speed with which the scenelets are intercut: the dialogue begins in a car, continues as the car is parked, continues through the car park, through the swing doors into hospital reception, along corridors, through scrubbing up and into the operating theatre, where the conversation turns to the medical work at hand. This is one continuous scene, broken up by location changes.

Structural imperatives – beginning, middle and end

When each play is 'complete' – i.e., all the scenes have been written – meaningful discussion on structure becomes possible. The opening of any narrative (the beginning of any drama) involves a disruption of the status quo: nothing happened before and everything happened before. Apparently. Such disruption of the narrative equilibrium is only possible to conceive because narrative is, in one sense, continuous and endless. The chunk of it which becomes the work of fiction is highlighted. It is, in a sense, all middle. The rest, before and after, is the not-written story. This is not about constructing 'back story', but rather about the importance of the choice of start and end points. Often this may not be clear until everything has been written. Even pre-planning cannot absolutely legislate for the 'correct' beginning. In any case the end will always determine (in some crucial way) the nature of the beginning.

The opening scene of John Osborne's *Look Back in Anger* is repeated in the household every week, when the men read the Sunday papers. However, this particular week is clearly different from the others, because it sets the 'story' of the play in motion. Sundays may have happened before in a generic sense, but this Sunday (to use McKee's phrase) is the 'inciting incident' for what follows. It is the prime cause, as it were, of which the rest of the play is the effect.

The end of every play heralds a resumption of order, some sort of invisible status quo, which is bound to be different from the status quo which has been disrupted at the start. Since nothing more is written, nothing appears to be happening afterwards. In reality, everything else happens afterwards, even though we have no evidence for what it is. The idea that any play can simply end by 'leaving the audience to make up their minds' is disingenuous.

The evidence in the play always tends to at least one possibility. Even if a storyline appears to be wrapped up – i.e., they live happily ever after – there are two possibilities which follow: first, they *do* live happily ever after and second, they *don't* live happily ever after. Evidence from within the play is likely to weigh towards one rather than the other, but it is always possible, of course, for two members of the audience to have different opinions, if different kinds of evidence (or even the same evidence) lead them to opposite conclusions. The end is never the end, any more than the beginning is ever the beginning. It is all middle. What is at stake here is the moment finally chosen by the dramatist to start the story and the moment chosen to end it.

Immediacy, pivot and exposition

The work done on lifting the words off the page helps students to understand what happens on the other side of the written text, as it were, by giving them a chance to experience what performers must do. At the same time it serves to elucidate and confirm the determining element of both writing and performance: the sense of immediacy, of the presentness of drama. Anyone watching drama instinctively engages in a structured experience of immediacy; the dramatist needs to make that awareness conscious and to translate it into dialogue, which always takes place in its own 'present' tenseness.

There is a creative writing cliché, which is sometimes adduced here: show, don't tell. Like all other clichés, this can be deconstructed to a point where it is not particularly useful as a clear guideline. For example, every story is a kind of 'telling'; in prose fiction, with the singular narrative voice, this is more obvious. In drama the 'telling' is oblique, conveyed through moving and speaking figures who appear to be showing as they go.

However, narrative 'telling', as it is inflected in prose fiction, can be entailed in drama through the medium or device of exposition. In earlier twentieth-century drama (the 'well-made play' syndrome) it was common to have an opening scene which self-consciously introduces the audience (gives the audience 'information') about relevant parts of the story so far. Often such information is supplied by secondary characters – servants, adjuncts to the main story. The opening speech of *The Second Mrs Tanqueray* by Arthur Wing Pinero, is a rather wonderful example of this:

MISQUITH Aubrey, it is a pleasant yet dreadful fact to contemplate, but it's nearly fifteen years since I first dined with you. You lodged in Piccadilly in those days, over a hat-shop. Jayne, I met you at that dinner, and Cayley Drummle.[2]

[2] *Trelawny of the Wells and other plays* by Arthur Wing Pinero (Oxford, 1995), p. 143.

All this information is primarily for the benefit of the audience since we can assume it is already known to the others. We can assume this because it comes right at the beginning and is not elicited in response to a question such as, 'Misquith, kindly remind me where we first met. I can't remember.' This kind of exposition, where information, provided from *within* the action, relevant only to the action, becomes a way to appear to leap over the fourth wall. Addressed directly to the audience, it is an example of concealed internal narrative.

Student writing often includes dialogue of this kind. Sometimes this takes the form of reported speech. The 'lesson' is to identify exposition which is outside the immediate moment of dramatic exchange. The incorporation of such exposition may constitute a form of note-taking by the dramatist in dialogue form. It is the kind of information which might be more at home in a synopsis or scenario. That does not mean the student should immediately go off and write a scenario; this may or may not be an appropriate thing to do at that moment. The most important thing is an awareness of the distinction between the immediate and response/reactive speech, and the less immediate. In any case all dialogue must, in the end, be structured round the illusion of its present-tenseness.

There is some useful work to be done exploring this. At the most basic level it involves demonstrating and analysing the difference between something which is happening 'now' and something which has happened in the past: this can be done by getting students to underline all verbs which are in the past tense:

JOHN   Would you like some scrambled eggs?
JANET   Yes, please. I haven't had scrambled eggs for ages.

Whatever Janet's line might express, or be prompted by – pleasure, enthusiasm, wistfulness – it bears a direct relation to John's question. However, it is not all a direct response to a direct question – for example, 'When did you last eat scrambled eggs?' It is, therefore, another kind of exposition, of information which comes from outside the immediacy of the moment. It is a reference to a moment in the past, when something else happened. If it is relevant to the present moment, it has an active function. If it is just incidental information, as it were, then it is (possibly) unnecessary exposition (unless it becomes important later).

After I have asked students to underline all the verbs in the past tense, we hear the scenes, read first in their entirety, then twice more: first with the present-tense sentences left out, then with the past-tense sentences left out. This is always exciting and illuminating – but again, it often takes students some time to comprehend and internalise the concept of exposition and its relationship to dramatic immediacy. The issue here is *not* about information leaping over the fourth wall, but rather to sharpen students' awareness of those moments where they may want to include reference to events outside the scene, and to be able to decide what and why. Information, of whatever kind, which does not belong to the dramatic immediacy of the moment and is not integral to the action (physical, narrative, emotional) can be demonstrated to be superfluous. Students must be able to discern, and internalise, the difference between the immediacy of the dramatic moment and all matter that is outside it.

There is a further exploration of exposition I often do. I suggest that each student should take two of his/her characters and write half a page of dialogue (taking five minutes to do it), in which each character only offers information in response to a question. This too is not always as straightforward as it might seem. It is not an 'exercise' in writing dialogue using questions, but in enhancing close focus on the way in which dialogue interacts, and then continues to accumulate and build. Every reaction (even a straight answer to a question) in dialogue is also a new action. Inevitably, dialogue always moves 'forward', generating more dialogue. This process of exploration also demonstrates the constant *reactiveness* of dialogue.

Example: narrative and causality

The following exchange of dialogue is the basis of an illustrative discussion of how scenes (narrative) are linked together, with some form of necessary sequencing or causality.

A   No eggs. No eggs. What do you mean by no eggs?
B   It is not my fault. It is the act of God.
A   Blasphemy. You tell me there are no eggs; and you blame your Maker for it.
B   What can I do? I cannot lay eggs.
A   No need to make a joke of it.
B   Well, we all have to do without eggs if the hens won't lay.
A   Now, you just listen to me.[3]

What is the relationship between these two people? Likely suggestions might be: a couple, a married couple. If asked why, someone might respond by saying that one person wants eggs for breakfast, which the other person is responsible for cooking. Where is the information about breakfast or cooking, I ask? There is no answer to that. However, it appears to be generally assumed that eggs stand in for 'breakfast'. The significant fact is that one person is in charge of knowledge about the eggs. With recourse to socially conventional roles, cultural assumptions, many people assume that since women tend to cook at home, that figure will be a woman and the other, therefore, will be a man. The text thus (a) reveals cultural assumptions, and (b) opens up alternative possibilities.

On the other hand it might not be a domestic scene at all, but a scene in a restaurant kitchen. The relationships, therefore, might be hierarchical – chef and waiter/waitress, for example. Evidence? Well, one person is more assertive, angrier, perhaps, than the other:

---

[3] Modified introductory dialogue from *Saint Joan* by George Bernard Shaw (Penguin, 1981), p. 49.

'Now, you just listen to me.' It could be two men or two women. They might be living together, because people have eggs for breakfast.

Whichever it finally turns out to be, there is clearly some kind of serious disagreement about eggs and their availability. Of course, in the long run eggs may turn out to be a metaphor for something quite else, even profound.

The scene is then examined for narrative, or story. What is suggested in this scene, which may already have happened? Evidence must be from the text. 'You tell me there are no eggs.' This could indicate that B has discovered already that there are no eggs. This is confirmed by 'We all have to go without eggs. The hens will not lay.' There is thus at least one scene that happened earlier, which could be written: who are the 'we' referred to here? Any person directly or indirectly referred to in a scene is a possible character for the play, since the person concerned is already important to one of the onstage people. 'I haven't had scrambled eggs for ages' suggests that the last time scrambled eggs were in evidence something important might have happened.

What about a possible following scene? For what are the eggs needed? We may have thought previously about eggs and breakfast, but if the attention is given to future events, the eggs might be needed for other things: guests arriving. A cake for a special event. The arrival of an important guest (a soufflé?), either the special event itself, or a scene of further preparation for the event. What is the event? There is another possible absent person who might be important for the play.

Structure

Say we are running three sequential scenes. I will 'spell' out the link between each scene – or will ask questions: Scene 1: A discovers there are no eggs for a daughter's twenty-first birthday party, and there is a confrontation between A and B, who is supposed to have got the eggs. Scene 2: B has managed to buy some duck eggs and suggests to A that the cake can be modified. A is intrigued at first, then unsure. Scene 3: B has finished the cake and asks A to decorate it. No one knows what eggs are in the cake.

Here Scene 2 follows Scene 1, since the duck eggs are a replacement for the hens' eggs, which we already know are not available. Scene 3 includes a cake, made with eggs of some kind. The cake could not be made until eggs had been obtained.

This is a perfectly sensible, logical, cause-and-effect order, in which each scene happens because of what has already happened in the scene(s) before. However, what happens if we change the order of the scenes? Not in order to 'improve' on the order we have, or because there is anything wrong with the order we already have. But just to see what effect changing the order might have on the narrative, on the order, sequence and implied cause-and-effect of the story.

We begin with Scene 3. A cake has been made. We then have Scenes 1 and 2. Leaving aside any odd lines or speeches that may not perfectly 'fit' this order, we look simply at the sequence of events. If Scene 1 follows a successful cake it might be that the first cake was a trial run, or for a less important event, thus highlighting the particular significance of the sudden failure in hens' egg provision. If, in what is now Scene 3, duck eggs are produced, the situation might be even worse, because the twenty-first birthday is of someone who is allergic to duck eggs.

By changing the order of the events a different storyline is suggested, because of the ways in which we might link events, suggesting cause and effect, or setting up parallel storylines, which will develop separately before they come together. Cause and effect can happen over long spans of time, as well as in short discernible spans. This is one of the ways in which suspense or tension is built in to the narrative.

Pivot

Each scene always has a pivotal moment, on which the rest of the scene depends. Or, to put it another way, without which the scene would have no rationale for being. This bears analogy with the concepts of beats and units, used by performers and directors. The pivot is always discovered only after the scene is written, after the event. It is not that every scene 'must' have a pivot. Every scene 'will' have a pivot, no matter what. In the exchange about eggs, the pivotal line is, 'What do you mean by no eggs?' Without this line, the rationale for the whole scene collapses.

13 Subject matter, character and follow-up

There are some topics, considered as fundamental to drama, which have not been treated in detail in this book. This is quite deliberate. The first is the area covered under the various terms of premise, idea, super-objective (see chapter 4). The second is character.

The premise/idea concept is virtually impossible to understand. As we have seen, it is a term interpreted in contradictory ways. It is taken to mean sometimes that the student needs to know everything about the drama before he/she starts writing dialogue – i.e., the story should already be structured; sometimes it means the message that is to emerge from the drama (what it 'says' or what the author wants to 'say'); sometimes it covers the theme (what it is 'about'). Clearly, each of these is an important issue, but equally, they are of limited use for the writing process. Some students will have a very strong notion of one or more of these, but others may not, either because they are genuinely unsure, or because they are not used to thinking in analytical, abstract ways.

Also, as with any other kind of writing, discursive or imaginative, however much or little one 'knows' before writing begins, new material always emerges during the writing and thinking process. Thinking about what one is thinking, writing, reading, rereading and rewriting is vital. But good intentions, or explicitly articulated intentionality, is never enough. Performing a literary-critical operation on one's own writing, to distil the message/theme/idea, is notoriously unstable as an activity. The necessary skills take a long time and a great deal of experience to develop. There is a tension between knowing as much as one possibly can about what one is doing, and the activities of reading and exegesis performed on the writing by someone else who is 'outside' the process.

Subject matter, theme and message

In class, I generate discussion of these important matters only and always after the event, after the short play is complete – or nearly complete. The entire play is run and we then elicit suggestions first for subject matter and then for theme. What is it about and what is it 'saying'? There are generally a number of suggestions in answer to both questions, with sufficient evidence from within the play to argue for any one. This is, of course, what critical interpretation is about. Subject matter, summarised in a single sentence, refers to elements in the narrative. So *Hamlet* is a play about royal succession. It is a play about a crisis in a mother-and-son relationship. It is a play about a man who cannot make up his mind. The theme of *Hamlet* is conscience. It is about ambition and greed. It is about the oppression of women, the way women are seen as passive. It is, whatever it is, an abstract noun. The message of *Hamlet* is respect your mother for being a person in her own right. It is that healthy government demands a close-knit family. It is that fate doth make cowards of us all. It is that brotherly love is a fine thing. It is some kind of moral, or polemic, or lesson. It could even be every single one of these all bound together.

Whatever it is, it is never one single idea or premise. Colloquially, one might say 'I have an idea for a play', but that could mean anything at all. It is most likely to mean simply that someone is ready to start writing a play. Students may already have 'ideas' when they come to a drama-writing class, but in the end it is what they write that counts. What they write in class may or may not be the most intimate expression of their soul, or even something they may feel passionately about, but that is, frankly, secondary to working with the convention, and acquiring the understanding and skills to do so. As has been briefly demonstrated, even the shortest snatch of dialogue already contains within it some narrative, the possibilities for a much longer narrative, relationships which compose the narrative, and a social world in which such a narrative takes place in the immediacy of the dramatic moment.

This is, of course, not to argue against those who find it productive to write a detailed synopsis, with a moment-by-moment scenario breakdown, before they begin to write dialogue. It is, however, to point out that doing so keeps the imaginative and writing processes within the bounds of prose and the work, in a sense, must begin all over again when dialogue is written.

The most productive way in the end is to move between the two, with the emphasis on dialogue; then, at a moment when there is already some substantial scenic material (in my classes at least three scenes), to draw back, think and plan, become aware of the overall timescale, the time gaps between scenes (if relevant), the total narrative, if it can be decided at this stage. Continue writing the drama (dialogue) and at intervals either repeat the analytical process, or leave it until the first version is finished, before analysing again. Structural and linguistic material thus constantly alternate and dovetail.

Character

Character is (forgive the metaphor) a can of worms. In earlier chapters I have discussed the way in which approaches to writing drama owe a great deal to critical approaches to the novel. Both the novel and post-Aristotelian approaches to drama often fall into the easy statement that the narrative is 'about' a hero or heroine, a central character. While there may be one such representation, which goes all the way through the story (i.e., Hamlet himself), he is never 'told' in isolation, but always in relationship.

I have argued that drama is not about writing 'character'. Even though each individuation must have a coherence, subscribe to appropriate registers in relation to the overall writing style of the dialogue, nevertheless, drama does not 'stem' from character, but consists rather of relationships and the events with which they are involved. There is no alternative in drama to writing relationships, while a novel may consist of narrated events or thoughts or feelings, which always remain within the perspective (and narrative voice) of individual figures. As was demonstrated in the diagrams (see chapter 10), the building of relationships is a complex, compounding matter.

In drama-writing how-to books students are asked to write biographies, sketches or backgrounds, providing a full history of their characters. Of course, there is a great deal which can be useful in information of this kind – the students must decide at some point whether their figures are male or female, roughly how old they are, what their situation in the world/family/relationships is etc. However, apart from the procrastinatory function of writing this as a prose biography, the fine details often do not settle until the narrative creates its own imperatives. As with the categories of subject matter and theme, I suggest writing a biographical sketch only *after* the event, when the play itself is complete. At that point the student only invents biographical information which is directly relevant to what happens in the play. Sometimes this stage will suggest some different imaginative possibility, which could influence the narrative and might be used for rewriting.

Rewriting and further writing

When students type up their work after class, I urge them not to do any major rewriting at home, or to extend the scene they have written. Small changes are fine. This is in order to keep the imaginative process to the structured class time. If, during the course of the semester or year, they want to write more, I encourage them to write whatever they want (of course) outside the class, thinking about the issues that come up in class and applying them to their writing. On structured courses, in any case, the assignment is likely to consist of a complete twenty-five- to thirty-minute drama, worked on independently.

If the course runs over more than one term/semester, I begin the second term with more freedom of choice for the students. I suggest that this time they might start their play from something (subject matter) they are sure they want to write about. This encourages conscious thinking and planning. Sometimes students will have clear ideas, sometimes they may not, until they have written a couple of scenes. Or a student might choose a historical subject or event, and read and research alongside his/her writing. This generates a process which involves a transformation of fact into fiction, or of mixing fact with fiction, as well as having to address the question of the language the student is using for the dialogue. Hamlet does not speak Danish and neither does he speak in medieval tropes. He speaks in Shakespearean iambic pentameter. If someone wants to write a version of *Hamlet*, will it be clothed in some contemporary street argot, will it be in free verse, will it be in landed-gentry strains? Whichever it is, the dialogue must always strive after the illusion of spontaneity.

After class

The class-based work I have described builds all the skills of writing drama gradually and cumulatively. Within a single semester/term it is possible to complete a short drama, which, in microcosm, covers all relevant issues, as well as allowing each student to develop her/his imaginative and writing skills. Dealing with the larger architectonic scope of a full-length drama, or even an hour-long piece, is much more difficult. It is analogous to the difficulty of 'teaching' the novel in creative writing classes. In both cases my approach is based on a long-standing educational principle that what is taught in class/seminar is thorough and comprehensive, and aims to provide the student with the intellectual and practical abilities to work independently. Students do not bring in longer work which is absorbing them at home. In other words, the class does not operate as some kind of impossible collective dramaturg to 'help' students to write their longer plays.

In this context there is much to be said in favour of encouraging students to meet separately in groups they organise themselves, if they want to bring in extracts from longer pieces on which they are working, hear fellow classmates lift the work off the page and even, if they want to, invite comments. This is best done without any teacher or tutor figure present; it enables students to apply analytical procedures independently (if they want to), or simply hear their work read out without comment.

During my classes I encourage students to see at least one stage drama during each term/semester. Pretty well everyone watches television anyway and many go to see films. But the experience of seeing a stage play enhances another aspect of the knowledge of immediacy. In an ideal world, students would return to see the same production two or three times, to mark similarities/differences in performance on different days with different audiences.

We take a short time – half an hour or so – to discuss the play they have seen. This is not a critic's review – it is not a discussion about whether they liked or disliked the play, whether they enjoyed it or not, whether they thought performances were 'good' or not. If someone does make a value judgement, it provides an opportunity to begin to investigate the criteria – the idea that performances must be 'convincing', 'believable', 'real' – that all hover behind the quick shorthand responses most people make to performance. The main push of the analysis in class is to encourage students to be able to settle completely into the enjoyable experience of watching a complete, seamless performance, while at the same time keeping the analytical part of their brains ticking over: separating the dialogue (the words they hear) from the way they are performed; from the way they have been directed; from the impact and effects of music, lighting, spectacle etc. It doesn't matter what the production is – it can be a lavish musical, or it might be a shoestring production in a room above a pub. It is the act of developing observation and analysis that is important. The ability to analyse what one sees increases the pleasure of the experience and gradually, over time, can be internalised and applied to the writing process itself.

14 Culture and representation

The issue of cultural representation has a particular urgency for those beginning to study the art of writing drama. This is not a return to the creative writing cliché that students 'must' write about and from their own personal experiences. The work on other languages, and the various Englishes available in any given group of students, is directly related to their own cultural, social, educational and ideological positioning, and therefore – in one way or another – this is part of their mental, intellectual and imaginative make-up. One of the consequences of an effective pedagogy in the art of writing drama should be to enable each student to reach a better and more productive understanding of his/her own imaginative resources. This is what enables students to reach a point where they can more consciously choose their own subject matter – a moment directly relevant to the drama they write for assignments, where they have complete freedom, and to any writing they may want to undertake in the future.

Language can be a route into cultural resources specific to each student, and lead to ways of writing dialogue which enable discussion of dialect, rhythm, pace, even what is commonly considered part of developing 'character', but character in and through relationships. It enables discussion of register and idiolect. In an ideal classroom world there should be time to read and discuss texts which deal with socio-linguistics. At the very least, each student stands a chance of having his/her imagination (perhaps even memories) expanded, to develop ideas about subject matter and the way in which this might be explored through writing drama.

This leads into areas of more trenchant understandings of socio-cultural positioning, as they impact on imaginative writing. Each student is, in some way, positioned as part of a class, ethnic, religious, gender-based group, and sometimes a complex combination of more than one of these categories. This is not to suggest that any one category is monolithic in itself, or that a crude line between (say) class and drama can predict the 'message' of such imaginative work. And, in the end, each student decides for him/herself whether issues of class, gender, ethnicity etc. interest him/her at a conscious level. What emerges from the imagination, subconsciously and unconsciously, may, of course, be quite another matter. It all comes down to the critical interpretation of the work, with evidence.

Gender as a case study

Discussion of the relationship between gender and drama is still, despite some of the benefits of feminism, necessary. Women writers were formative in the development of the novel and its readership, during the eighteenth and nineteenth centuries. In this century women novelists have a relatively secure place as producers of fiction. In drama, however, the story is very different. Gender distinctions, balances and imbalances, operate in all cultural and social groups, and each has its own interests and perspectives to bring to the art of writing drama.

Feminism in the 1970s drew attention to gender imbalance

[1] *Carry On, Understudies; theatre and sexual politics* by Michelene Wandor (Routledge, 1986). First published in 1981. *Post-War British Drama: Looking Back in Gender* by Michelene Wandor (Routledge, 2001). First published 1987. *Plays by Women*, ed. Michelene Wandor (Methuen, 1982–5).

throughout the theatre industry.[1] A compendious list of plays written by women consisted of over 400 entries for women playwrights from the tenth to the twenty-first century, showing that, gender imbalance notwithstanding, many women had written plays.[2] Even so, women dramatists figure as a minority in the professional dramatic media, just as they do as artistic directors of theatres – a survey in 1984 found that only 12 per cent of artistic directors were women and while the figure had risen in 2006 to around 19 per cent, the situation still demands attention.[3]

Women dramatists

Aristocratic women wrote courtly masques, but it was not until actresses appeared on the Restoration stage in the late seventeenth century that women began writing for the stage professionally – the best-known of these is Aphra Behn, who is popularly seen as Britain's first professional woman dramatist. Women dramatists have come into prominence during moments of historical and cultural change: during the Restoration, when actresses were for the first time officially welcomed/allowed on to the stage; in the early part of the twentieth century during the women's suffrage movement; then again in the 1970s during the second wave of feminism. Many of the plays written for the Actresses' Franchise League (founded in 1908) were produced by the actresses themselves, because they wanted new material. During the 1930s sisters Angela and Joan Tuckett wrote and produced plays on women's rights, as part of Unity Theatre's socialist theatre programme.

The situation of women playwrights bears a close relationship to the position of women in the theatre industry at large. The sexual division of labour operates in a pyramid-shaped structure, where men dominate both at the apex and at the base, in the technological

[2] *She Also Wrote Plays* by Susan Croft (Faber, 2001).
[3] Lyn Gardner, 'It's time we got angrier', *Guardian*, 4 April 2007.

and manual labour areas of backstage production, as well as at the artistic 'top', making major executive decisions about the dramatists who are commissioned, the plays produced and the subject matter staged.

Women working in the theatre industry (apart from actresses) tend to cluster in the middle of the pyramid. Although since the nineteenth century there has been a strong tradition of women costume and set designers, the top professional designers are almost all male. Women tend to work in areas which reflect 'servicing' roles similar to those in other industries, and in the domestic division of labour – the housekeeping parts of theatre: secretarial, administration, assisting, personnel, casting, wardrobe, publicity. The pattern is similar in the film and television industries. All these jobs are, of course, vital and highly skilled, but they are also jobs which are largely behind the scenes, not particularly well paid and rarely given the credit they deserve, whether staffed by men or women.

The figures for women playwrights, judged on the basis of produced and published drama, are depressing. In 1985 Methuen, the main drama publisher in this country, listed eighty twentieth-century dramatists, of whom seven were women; just under 10 per cent. In 1999 Methuen's catalogue showed an increase in published women playwrights, up to 15 per cent. Also in 1999, in the catalogue of drama published by Nick Hern Books, the percentage of plays by women dramatists was around 12 per cent. A selective survey of plays running over two weeks in 2006 showed little change in the gender balance.[4]

There is also a related knock-on effect in terms of subject matter, 'character' distribution, and therefore the relative employment opportunities for male and female performers. In Methuen's catalogue in 1985, information was given for the male–female ratio of characters in the plays: 2,212 male characters and 908 female characters. While it is not necessarily the case that women

[4] 'Women in Theatre Survey', Sphinx Theatre Company, 2006.

dramatists will write more parts for women, the real point is that this kind of statistic actually does confirm that, despite the fact that drama schools tend to be careful to take equal numbers of male–female students, the women will have a much harder time finding jobs and will, on average, earn far less than their male counterparts (star salaries notwithstanding). The gender balance, in terms of the gender-based content of plays, is very strongly male-weighted.

This results in (acknowledged or not) an imaginatively male-gendered perspective in both narrative and theme or message. It affects the ways in which women are 'represented' in plays as characters, and the ways in which the gendered human agencies in drama drive and focus the action, dialogue and relationships. In this sense the content and perspective, the multiple-voiced points of view, of drama are ideologically 'policed' far more explicitly than the content of novels, since plays are only published once they have achieved some interest and/or success in performance. Thus the composition and operation of the theatre industry itself has a more direct impact on how many women dramatists are commissioned, encouraged and, effectively, 'allowed' to make a professional career as dramatists. By analogy, the same will apply to male and female dramatists from other cultural groups and, indeed, to the relatively small number of dramas written by men *and* women from other cultural groups in general.

When it comes to plays for the thriving amateur dramatic movement in the UK things are different. Amateur companies often produce plays which have been successful in the professional theatre, but there is also a large market for plays especially written for amateur performance. Samuel French specialise in this area, with plays for mixed casts, all-female and all-male casts. Their catalogue of plays for the amateur market overall reveals about 15 per cent of the writers as female, except for the category of one-act plays for all-female casts, where about half the plays are by women dramatists.

It is clear from this that there is something of a decisive performing amateur/professional divide. At amateur level there are more performing actresses than actors; at professional level the opposite is true. More women write plays for the amateur market, especially where they have all-female casts, but male writers dominate in both spheres.

The public nature of the dramatist's 'publication' has some bearing on the choices writers make about where they will work. A dramatist may be present during rehearsal for at least some of the time and may, in any case, confer with the director during the rehearsal period. Rehearsals may involve changes, modification, explanation, justification, sometimes exciting, sometimes difficult and painful, often defensive. This is a more public (not collaborative) procedure than the relatively private editorial relationship between, say, a novelist and a publisher's editor. The dramatist thus needs to 'come out', as it were. She/he cannot hide behind, or take refuge behind the safety of the published text. The dramatist's name will appear outside the theatre, on leaflets, on posters. In movies the writer's name will be much smaller, appearing after the stars and (often) the director.

For a woman dramatist to take on this kind of public authoritative voice (a voice with authority, but without executive power) means that in some way she will, de facto, be challenging the dominant image of the male as moral, literary and aesthetic arbiter. However conservative or anti-feminist she might be, however she might think or believe that there is no longer any need for feminism any more, her empirical presence as a woman playwright puts her in a minority, a relative exception who proves the rule.

There is an interesting, aesthetic, formal literary reason why it may be harder for women to opt for writing drama. Writing drama involves not only finding a 'voice' in a characteristic, distinctive literary sense, in what is called the 'style' of each dramatist. Writing drama entails dialogue, which even at its most introverted moment creates social interactive action. The dramatist makes inner private voices become public utterances, invents public interaction and creates active, effective relationships. The dramatist does not have recourse to the private-seeming world of single-person narrative, with access to the inner, invisible consciousness.

A woman dramatist is potentially in a very powerful position. She animates a staged public world in which there are multiple voices, engaging with each other, inventing and creating an imagined world and its history, creating and controlling the voices of others (the characters, the performers), while developing her own literary style, interests and stamp. She is controlling the voices of others who speak in public, while, paradoxically, having little public voice in her own cultural right, as a woman.

Our public cultural world still does not accept or sufficiently encourage women to give public voice, for reasons which relate to long-standing gender taboos on public speaking and holding public authority. We only need to think of the news, day after day and evening after evening, showing male politicians in interchangeable grey suits pronouncing on issues which concern us all, male and female. As academic Cora Kaplan wrote, 'Public writing and public speech, closely allied, were both real and symbolic acts of self-determination for women.'[5] Although Kaplan was writing about women in the nineteenth century and although things have shifted somewhat, we are very far from parity, socially and culturally, in the power of the female voice in public. This is critical to the backdrop against which any dramatic writing may be taught.

A woman dramatist is still reacted to as a woman as much as, or sometimes more than, she is as a writer. A woman dramatist has more to overcome before she can be accepted as an artistic 'equal' in the dramatic worlds of production. Artistic directors who run theatres and make decisions, even sometimes women artistic directors, are often operating a hidden agenda in which the norms

[5] Introduction to the reprint of *Aurora Leigh* by Elizabeth Barrett Browning (The Women's Press, 1978), p. 9.

of important subject matter, as well as literary capacity, are still determined by men, or by points of view determined by men: the decision about what is considered proper or interesting or important subject matter.

Like other creative writing classes, drama-writing classes tend to have more women than men in them. Their relative invisibility at professional level contrasts with this fact, as it does with their participation in amateur theatre. While the case study of gender in relation to writing drama demands attention in its own right, it is a vital indicator of ways in which similar understandings need to be developed in relation to other kinds of cultural resources. It is part of the ongoing struggle to increase cultural representation to match that of our demographic cultural reality, and has a particularly vital role to play in the representation of dramatic writing and in work with students to foster the art of writing drama.

15 Conclusions

Anyone can write dialogue; we all have conversations, real and imagined. Writing drama, however, is something else. It is dialogue, aesthetically shaped into the conventions of the dramatic genre, involving choices which may be unthinking, unconscious and spontaneous. It produces drama which then can have another existential life as a performance artefact. The dramatic media came into being without schools of dramatic writing and will no doubt continue quite happily in the same way – constantly inundated with scripts from enthusiastic and ambitious people. To put it frankly, the dramatic media are not dependent on courses in the art of writing drama. Nor, it must be said, will the presence of such courses necessarily produce new geniuses of the dramatic art. The primary purpose of a course in the art of writing drama is to deepen an understanding of the genre from a writerly perspective, for each student to develop her/his own practical skills, and to understand what is involved in the distinctive journey between imagination, page and stage.

Each of the chapters in this book approaches this project from a slightly different angle, and is consciously addressed to teachers and students and to the dramatic media. I am very aware that teaching imaginative writing in any genre, on its own, separate from a study of the history of the genre, its typologies, its theoretical and critical approaches, is a partial activity. Teaching drama writing shares in many of the contradictions which currently surround creative writing in general. At the same time, it is one of the most exciting new arrivals in the academy.

Imaginative writing can be, and is being, taught. The art of writing drama can be, and is being, taught in universities, in adult education, in film schools and some theatres. However, it cannot be detached from its cultural and intellectual contexts: a study of dramatic history and its products (plays and scripts), a study of the performance media which interest the student (theatre, film, TV, radio), the critical and theoretical writing which addresses these, and the mercurial, exciting material and illusory object that is performance itself. Writing drama is one part of this cluster. In adult education students enjoy the benefits of just choosing courses they want to take; higher education has a more serious responsibility, to provide critical and contextual studies into which the art of writing drama fits.

Bibliography

Archer, William, *Play-making: a manual of craftsmanship* (Chapman & Hall, 1912)

Arden, John, *To Present the Pretence* (Eyre Methuen, 1977)

Aristotle, *Poetics* (Everyman, 1941)

Artaud, Antonin (trans. Victor Corti), *The Theatre and its Double* (Calder & Boyars, 1970)

Aston, Elaine and Savona, George, *Theatre as Sign-System: a Semiotics of Text and Performance* (Routledge, 1998)

Austin, J. L., *How to do Things with Words* (Harvard University Press, 1975)

Ayckbourn, Alan, *The Crafty Art of Playmaking* (Faber, 2002)

Baker, George Pierce, *Dramatic Technique* (Da Capo, 1976)

Barker, Howard, *Arguments for a Theatre* (Manchester, 1993)

Barthes, Roland, *Image, Music, Text* (Fontana, 1977)

Battersby, Christine, *Gender and Genius* (The Women's Press, 1994)

Bennett, Susan, *Theatre Audiences* (Routledge, 2003)

Bentley, Eric, *The Life of the Drama* (Applause, 1991)

Bentley, Eric (ed.), *The Theory of the Modern Stage* (Penguin, 1968)

Berry, Cicely, *Text in Action* (Virgin, 2001)

Blau, Herbert, *The Audience* (Johns Hopkins University Press, 1990)

Braun, Edward, *The Director and the Stage* (Methuen, 1983)

Brook, Peter, *The Empty Space* (Penguin, 1977)

Burns, Elizabeth and Tom, *Sociology of Literature and Drama* (Penguin, 1973)

Byron, Glennis, *Dramatic Monologue* (Routledge, 2003)

Carlson, Marvin, *Performance* (Routledge, 2003)

Carlson, Marvin, 'Indexical Space in the Theatre', in *ASSAPH Studies in the Theatre*, section C, no. 10 (Faculty of Visual and Performing Arts, Tel Aviv University, 1994)

Castagno, Paul C., *New Playwriting Strategies* (Routledge, 2001)

Chambers, Colin, *The Story of Unity Theatre* (Lawrence & Wishart, 1989)

Counsell, Colin, *Signs of Performance* (Routledge, 1996)

Counsell, Colin and Wolf, Laurie, *Performance Analysis* (Routledge, 2001)

Cowgill, Linda J., *Secrets of Screenplay Structure* (Lone Eagle, 1999)

Croft, Susan, *She Also Wrote Plays* (Faber, 2001)

Dessen, Alan C. and Thomson, Leslie, *A Dictionary of Stage Directions in English Drama, 1580–1642* (Cambridge University Press, 2000)

Donellan, Declan, *The Actor and the Target* (Nick Hern Books, 2005)

Eagleton, Terry, *Marxism and Literary Criticism* (Methuen, 1976)

Edgar, David, *The Second Time as Farce* (Lawrence & Wishart, 1988)

Edgar, David (ed.), *State of Play* (Faber, 1999)

Edgar, David, 'The Canon, the Contemporary and the New', in Reitz, Bernhard and Stahl, Heiko (eds), *What Revels are at Hand* (Wissenschaftlicher Verlag Trier, 2001)

Egri, Lajos, *The Art of Dramatic Writing* (Isaac Pitman, 1950)

Elam, Keir, *The Semiotics of Theatre and Drama* (Methuen, 1980)

Esslin, Martin, *The Field of Drama* (Methuen, 1988)

Esslin, Martin, *The Theatre of the Absurd* (Penguin, 1968)

Fortier, Mark, *Theory/Theatre* (Routledge, 1997)

Fuchs, Elinor, *The Death of Character* (Indiana University Press, 1996)

Gerould, Daniel (ed.), *Theatre/Theory/Theatre* (Applause, 2000)

Gooch, Steve, *Writing a Play* (A & C Black, 2004)

Greig, Noel, *Playwriting* (Routledge, 2005)

Griffiths, Stuart, *How Plays are Made* (Spectrum, 1984)

Hayman, Ronald, *How to Read a Play* (Grove Press, 1977)

Holquist, Michael, *Dialogism: Bakhtin and his World* (Routledge, 1990)

Howard, Pamela, *What is Scenography?* (Routledge, 2002)

Italie, Jean-Claude van, *The Playwright's Workbook* (Applause, 1997)

Johnstone, Keith, *Impro for Storytellers* (Faber, 1999)

Keyssar, Helene, *Feminist Theatre and Theory* (Macmillan, 1996)

Lawson, John Howard, *Theory and Technique of Playwriting* (Putnam's, 1949)

Levy, Shimon and Yaari, Nurit, 'Theatrical Responses to Political Events: the Trojan War on the Israeli Stage during the Lebanon War, 1982–1984' (*Journal of Theatre and Drama*, vol. 4, 1998, University of Haifa)

Lodge, David, *The Practice of Writing* (Secker & Warburg, 1996)

Mamet, David, *Three Uses of the Knife* (Vintage Books, 2000)

Mamet, David, *True and False* (Vintage, 1999)

McKee, Robert, *Story* (Methuen, 1999)

Melrose, Susan, *A Semiotics of the Dramatic Text* (Macmillan, 1994)

Mitter, Shomit, *Systems of Rehearsal* (Routledge, 2005)

Monteith, Moira and Miles, Robert (eds.), *Teaching Creative Writing* (Open University Press, 1992)

Nelson, Richard and Jones, David (ed. Colin Chambers), *Making Plays* (Faber, 1995)

Nicoll, Allardyce, *The English Theatre* (Nelson, 1936)

Osborne, John, *Look Back in Anger* (Faber, 1996)

Page, Adrian (ed.), *The Death of the Playwright* (Macmillan, 1992)

Pavis, Patrice, *Languages of the Stage* (Performing Arts Journal Publications, 1993)

Pike, Frank and Dunn, Thomas G., *The Playwright's Handbook* (Plume, Penguin, NY, 1996)

Reinelt, Janelle G., and Roach, Joseph R. (eds), *Critical Theory and Performance* (University of Michigan Press, 1996)

Rowell, George and Jackson, Anthony, *The Repertory Movement* (Cambridge University Press, 1984)

Russell Taylor, John, *Anger and After* (Eyre Methuen, 1977)

Russell Taylor, John, *The Second Wave* (Eyre Methuen, 1978)

Sanger, Keith, *The Language of Drama* (Routledge, 2001)

Schechner, Richard, *Performance Theory* (Routledge, 2003)

Searle, John R., *Expression and Meaning* (Cambridge University Press, 1994)

Searle, John R., *Speech Acts* (Cambridge University Press, 1969)

Shepherd, Simon and Wallis, Mick, *Drama/Theatre/Performance* (Routledge, 2004)

Shepherd, Simon and *Wells, Mick, Studying Plays* (Edward Arnold, 1998)

Smily, Sam (with Norman A. Bert), *Playwriting* (Yale University Press, 2005)

Spencer, Stuart, *The Playwright's Guidebook* (Faber, 2002)

Sphinx Theatre Company, *Women in Theatre Survey* (Sphinx Theatre Company, 2006)

Stanislavsky, Constantin (trans. Elizabeth Reynolds Hapgood), *An Actor Prepares* (Methuen, 2006)

Styan, J. L., *The English Stage* (Cambridge University Press, 1996)

Taylor, Val, *Stage Writing* (Crowood Press, 2002)

Tierno, Michael, *Aristotle's 'Poetics' for Screenwriters: Storytelling Secrets from the Greatest Mind in Western Civilisation* (Hyperion, 2002)

Wagner, Betty Jane, *Dorothy Heathcote: Drama as a Learning Medium* (Hutchinson, 1985)

Wandor, Michelene, *Carry on, Understudies: theatre and sexual politics* (Routledge, 1986)

Wandor, Michelene, *Post-War British Drama: Looking Back in Gender* (Routledge, 2001)

Wandor, Michelene, *The Author is not Dead, Merely Somewhere Else* (Palgrave Macmillan, 2008)

Willett, John, *The Theatre of Bertolt Brecht* (Eyre Methuen, 1977)

Willett, John (trans.), *Brecht on Theatre* (Hill and Wang, 1964)

Williams, Raymond, *Writing in Society* (Verso, 1991)

Williams, Raymond, *Drama from Ibsen to Brecht* (Penguin, 1976)

Williams, Raymond, *Drama in Performance* (Penguin, 1972)

Yeger, Sheila, *The Sound of One Hand Clapping* (Amber Lane Press, 1990)